Present from th

A play

Richard Everett

Samuel French — London
New York - Toronto - Hollywood

PRESENT FROM THE PAST

First performed at the Watermill Theatre, Newbury, on 5th May 1992, with the title *Hindsight*. The cast was as follows:

Howard	Richard Kane
Frances	Fiona Hendley
Rachel	Kay Adshead
Colin	John Conroy
David	Morris Perry

Director Euan Smith
Designer Mark Bailey
Lighting David I Taylor

Subsequently revived for a national tour in 1993 by Rod Coton Ltd, with the title *Present from the Past*. The cast was as follows:

Howard	Geoffrey Davies
Frances	Rula Lenska
Rachel	Patricia Brake
Colin	John Conroy
David	Derek Waring

Director Euan Smith
Designer Geoffrey Scott
Lighting Chris Nicholls

COPYRIGHT INFORMATION

(See also page ii)

CHARACTERS

Howard, 40s
Frances, 40
Rachel, early 40s
Colin, mid-40s
David, 69

The action takes place in the living-room, hall and stairs
of a terraced house in south-west London

The action is continuous

Time — the present

ACT I

The ground floor living-room, hall and stairs of a terraced house in south-west London

A door leads to a partly seen kitchen which in turn leads to the garden. Next to the door is a sash window. There is a narrow hall to one side leading to the stairs, the front room door and, at the end, the front door

It is evident that this is the home of an elderly person. The atmosphere of the house is a little drab but by no means cold or unwelcoming; it is merely well lived-in. The living-room is tidy but cluttered, full of photographs, books and assorted family memorabilia. The focal point of the room is a wing chair with a small table beside it; a bureau desk, with papers in it, stands to one side. There is a sofa as well. In the hall there is a telephone table with a telephone and notepad on top of it and various directories on the shelves below

When the CURTAIN *rises the living-room curtains are closed and all the doors are shut. A shaft of sunlight strikes across the room from between the curtains. The house is still. A newspaper and pen lie on the seat of the wing chair and a cup and saucer stand on the table. Various newspapers, circulars and assorted pieces of useless debris clutter the floor by the front door*

We hear the sound of keys turning in a lock... and then another one. The front door opens slightly and then has to be forced because of the papers that have accumulated beneath it. Howard enters, carrying a small bag. He is in his forties and, although he is smartly dressed in a dark suit and overcoat, he has a shambling quality about him. He walks slowly along the hall and tentatively opens the door into the living-room. He enters the room and pauses. He looks across at the wing chair and then picks up the cup and saucer on the table beside it; he holds them for a moment and then replaces them carefully. He picks up the newpaper and pen, examining and then replacing them, being careful to arrange them exactly as they were. He contemplates the room

Frances enters through the front door. She is aged forty, and is well-dressed and stylish both in turn-out and manner. In addition to a shoulder hand-bag, she has an overnight bag with her. A pair of spectacles hangs on a chain around her neck

Frances Howard?
Howard Frances?

Frances enters the living-room

Ah. There you are.
Frances (*reacting to the smell of the house*) Poof!
Howard Yes, I know. It does a bit.

Frances draws the curtains open and wrestles with the window, trying to open it

Frances Rachel not here yet?
Howard Um ... No. Not yet.
Frances (*breaking her nail*) Ow! Damn it ... You have a try.

Howard takes over trying to open the window, thumping it several times

(*Taking in the room*) Bit of a state, isn't it?
Howard Yes, well, as I said on the phone: nothing's been touched.
Frances Sorry to hold things up.
Howard Oh, good heavens — we understood. (*He opens the window*) Ah, that's got it. Splendid. Get some air in the place. We used to climb through here, remember?
Frances Did we?
Howard Yes. At night in our pyjamas, while Mother was sitting in her chair ... Anyway, how are you?

They kiss each other on the cheek

Frances Fine, yes. Sorry to have lumbered you with it all.
Howard Oh, nonsense. The undertakers did most of it — and a bunfight at Rachel's afterwards. No, no — what else could you do? Caribbean, wasn't it?
Frances St Lucia, yes.
Howard How very nice. You look jolly good on it, too.
Frances Thank you.
Howard Jolly good, yes. So. Bit of a sad moment, really.
Frances Yes.
Howard The end of a chapter and all that.
Frances Yes.
Howard Still. Doesn't do to get all ——
Frances No.

Howard No. So. You had a good time, then?
Frances Lovely.
Howard Good. That's good. When did you get back?
Frances Last Monday week.
Howard Oh, a while ago.
Frances Ten days. A mountain of things waiting for me.
Howard Yes. Isn't it always the way? And, by the time you've sorted through, you need another holiday to recover. How's it going, that interior design thing?
Frances Very well. Everyone wants a new bathroom, it seems.
Howard Do they? Marvellous.
Frances Can't get themselves clean enough, apparently. Something to do with guilt. What about you?
Howard Me? Fine. My bathroom's in terrific shape.
Frances I meant, Bristol. Business. Booming, is it?
Howard Yes. Rather too well, as it happens: I've been taken over.
Frances Oh. Do quite nicely out of that, won't you?
Howard I expect so. There's the small matter of how to occupy my time, of course.
Frances Won't you stay on?
Howard They asked me but, as everyone said, no point in being at the wheel if you're not allowed to steer.
Frances No. Still. You'll find something.
Howard Oh, yes. The world's my oyster, as they say.
Frances Should we make a start, d'you think, or wait for Rachel?
Howard May as well wait. Traffic, probably.
Frances Have you been upstairs?
Howard Not yet. I thought if we assembled here, the three of us, then we can go through systematically.
Frances Right ... Shouldn't take long, anyway.
Howard No, no. Poor old thing.
Frances I'm sure it was quick, though.
Howard What was? Oh ... yes.
Frances These things usually are.
Howard Oh, yes. I was noticing the crossword, earlier.
Frances Really?
Howard All but the last clue.
Frances Really. There we are, then — quick as anything. Come on, Rachel, where are you?
Howard Look ... um ... I've brought some clothes to hop into, here — in case there's any digging about needed ...
Frances How d'you mean?
Howard Cupboards and so forth — so I may as well ... (*He looks about*) Let's see ...

Frances D'you want me to ... ?
Howard No, that's all right. I'll ... um ... I'll nip upstairs — a last change in
the old bedroom. You'll be all right down here, will you?
Frances Fine. I'll keep an eye out for Rachel.
Howard Fine. Shan't ... er ... shan't be long, then.

Howard exits up the stairs

*Frances perches on the arm of the wing chair. She reaches down, picks up
the newspaper and pen and then puts on her spectacles. She looks at the
crossword, counts on her fingers, and then writes in some letters. She
discards the newspaper and picks up the cup and saucer*

*Repulsed by the cup's contents, Frances speedily exits to the kitchen with
it*

*Rachel enters briskly through the front door. She is a homely sort in her
early forties, dressed in sensible, uninspired clothes. She has two carrier
bags with her*

Rachel Hallo?

Frances enters from the kitchen

Frances In here, Rachel!

Rachel enters the living-room, breathlessly. They kiss

Rachel Hi, Fran ... God! Look at you! Wonderful!
Frances Thank you.
Rachel Really ... fabulous.

She bustles off through to the kitchen

(*Off*) I'll just put the kettle on and then we can start! Sorry I'm late! Stuck
on the tube for twenty minutes — someone thrown themselves on the line,
apparently!

She enters from the kitchen

Where's our big brother, then?
Frances Upstairs.

Rachel returns to the kitchen, saying the following as she goes

Rachel I've brought some milk, by the way.
Frances Well done.
Rachel (*off*) Shouldn't take long, should it?
Frances I hope not. Someone's picking me up later; we've a plane to catch.

Rachel appears once more

Rachel Because I've got to get back for the children's tea ... God, you do look
fabulous, Fran, hardly recognize you. Where was it, again?
Frances St Lucia.
Rachel St Lucia, that was it. I went through all the saints and couldn't
remember. Colin's trying for Brittany, this year.
Frances Brittany. What fun.
Rachel Should be — if he can mend the camper in time ... (*She goes into the
hall*)

*Howard appears on the stairs; he has changed his clothes and is carrying
his suit on a hanger*

Howard? ... Ah, there you are.
Howard Jolly good — you made it.

*Howard and Rachel hug affectionately, patting each other's backs. The hug
is prolonged through the following dialogue*

Rachel Mmmmh ... a sad, sad day.
Howard I know — but we mustn't be maudlin about it.
Rachel No, no.
Howard She wouldn't have wanted that.
Rachel She wouldn't.

They break from the hug

So ... How are you, then?
Howard Fine. Never better. You?
Rachel Oh, you know: battling on ...

*Rachel returns to the kitchen, banging about with crockery etc., under the
following dialogue. Howard and Frances exchange knowing smiles as
Rachel prattles on*

(*Off*) Tricia's got a boyfriend. Ha! Gone are the days of a lingering peck
on the doorstep, I tell you — looks more like they're having lunch to me.
Jamie's taken up permanent residence in the bathroom, in search of the lost

whisker and zit-busting, and little Mandy's passed Grade One Piano, bless her. Who'd be an afterthought, eh?

She enters from the kitchen again

What about Fran, then — have you seen the colour of her, your sister?

Howard I have, I know. I'm surprised she got through immigration.

Frances Good ... Well, as we're all here, shall we begin?

Rachel Yes. Now, I've brought some bin-liners — black for Oxfam, green for us.

Frances Oxfam? I thought you'd arranged for some house-clearers.

Rachel We have.

Frances Tomorrow.

Rachel Yes.

Frances Then it's a quick check round for anything valuable and that's it, isn't it?

Howard This isn't a smash-and-grab raid, Frances.

Frances I know it isn't — of course it isn't.

Howard (*picking up the newspaper*) What's this?

Frances What's what?

Rachel The crossword, bless her — at least she managed to finish it.

Howard She didn't, actually.

Frances No, I did.

Howard What?

Frances Just now.

Howard Frances, we haven't set foot in the place. Rachel and I specifically waited for you to get back.

Frances I know.

Howard Nothing's been touched.

Frances I know, Howard, you told me.

Rachel Tea. That's what we all need.

Rachel exits to the kitchen. There is a brief pause

Howard Sorry.

Frances My fault.

Howard It's just that I saw it there earlier — just as she'd left it and ... Stupid. It's only a damn crossword.

Frances Quite. Don't go all Gothic on us, please.

Howard I'm not, no. It's odd, that's all. Feels so odd, having grown up here, never having been here without her in it, it feels so ... well, I don't know how to put it, really ....

Frances Odd.

Howard Yes, you find that? I certainly find that.
Frances Not really. And I shouldn't dwell on it.

Rachel enters with a tray of tea things

Rachel Here we are. I found some sugar. You take sugar, Howard, don't you?
Howard Yes.
Rachel You don't, Fran, I know that.
Frances I've got my own.
Rachel Oh, I tried those pill things; left a horrible taste.
Frances They do the job, though.
Rachel If you say so. Colin says I shouldn't bother: a lost cause, he says ... "I'm the only one that sees it", he says, "so, if it helps, I won't look." (*She hands Howard a cup of tea*) There we are, treasure. (*She hands a cup to Frances*) Oh, I should have brought biscuits — stupid. Well, then — cheers or whatever.

They stand awkwardly in a row sipping tea

Frances Shall we make a start, then?
Rachel Oh, I knew there was something. On my way here I was thinking — don't laugh, you'll probably think I'm being silly — but, I was thinking ... it would be rather nice — well, appropriate — if we said a little prayer, really: what do you think?

Howard and Frances look embarrassed

Frances What for? I mean ... why — exactly?
Rachel Well ... she was our mother and with you missing the funeral, Fran, I just thought ... perhaps not. Silly idea.
Howard Not at all, if that's what you'd like.
Rachel Don't do it for me. It's not for me.
Frances Who, then?
Rachel Leave it. Forget it.
Frances No, come on.
Rachel I said "No", Frances.
Frances Rachel ... we'll say a prayer.
Rachel Right, then. Ready, Howard?
Howard Yes.

They stand uneasily in a line, heads bowed over their cups of tea. There is a brief pause

Rachel Who's going to start?

Frances Just say a prayer, Rachel.

Rachel I don't know any prayers — well, I do but I don't ...

Frances God ... "For what we are about to receive ..."

Rachel Not that one, Fran! You can't say that at a time like this. You do it, Howard. What was that one we used to say as children: "Bless our home and something something ——"

Frances (*rattling it off*) "Watch over us as we pray. Keep our hearts and minds ——"

Rachel Yes, that's it, that's the one — off you go, Howard.

Howard "Lord, bless our home and ——"

Rachel Hold on, let's put these down. I feel funny holding a cup and saucer.

They all put their cups and saucers down

Right. Sorry, Howard.

Howard "Lord, bless our home ——"

Rachel Are we joining in, or is Howard ...?

Frances Oh, do let's get on with it, shall we?

Rachel On the count of three, then: one ... two ...

Rachel
Howard } (*together*) { "Lord, bless our home and those within it, watch over us we pray. Keep our hearts and minds at
Frances peace, 'til night becomes the day."

Frances Amen. Now, shall we begin upstairs or down here? I tell you what — if we do a room each, we'll be through a hell of a lot quicker. What do you think, Howard?

Rachel (*removing a housecoat from one of her bags and pulling it on*) I'm worried about your clothes, Fran. Have you brought something to put over that?

Howard saunters over to the bureau desk

Frances No, I'll be fine ... Howard?

Rachel Oh, don't be silly. There's Mum's old pinny ——

Frances Please, Rachel, don't fuss.

Rachel Come on, I'll find ——

Frances All right! I'll get the damn pinny.

Frances exits into the kitchen

Howard looks through some papers

Rachel It was nice to do that. I'm glad we did that.

Howard Mmmh?

Rachel Saying a prayer. You didn't mind, did you?

Howard Of course not. Why should I mind?

Rachel Terrible — your head goes a complete blank. It's like in church; it's all the modern stuff now, at our place. When we first started going I was in such a muddle; I was busily "thou-ing" and "trespassing" while everyone else was "you-ing" and "sinning".

Howard Church?

Rachel Oh, not — you know — nothing serious. Mandy's fault, being a Brownie. Once a month they all go for church parade, and the vicar's nice, very young, plays a guitar, not electric or anything. Anyway, Colin quite likes it and they have real bread and not wafers which I think's rather nice. Mind you, it's wholemeal and Colin says it sticks in his teeth; he's going to raise it at the PCC.

Frances appears from the kitchen wearing an old pinny. She makes a lame attempt at adjusting her appearance in the mirror

Frances Right. All set, then?

Rachel Oh, lovely.

Frances Thank you. Think it's me do you, Rachel?

Rachel Oh, definitely.

Frances All I need now are three snotty kids and a pile of ironing. Ha! Right. I'll take the bedroom, you take the spare room, Rachel — Howard, what about you?

Howard Shouldn't we be doing this together?

Rachel We are. What d'you mean?

Howard The three of us, a room at a time.

Frances God, no, it'll take forever. We'll split up and work through. I've brought some labels for anything large, the smaller stuff we can put on one side.

Howard Stuff?

Frances Yes. Is that all right with you two?

Howard Not really. There's a lot here and I think ——

Frances Look, Howard. Rachel's brood need feeding and I've got a plane to catch.

Rachel Where to this time?

Frances Just Paris, for the weekend — someone's picking me up. So let's get the job done and go, shall we?

Howard Frances ——

Frances I'm not sitting in the Champs-Elysées smelling of death, Howard, OK? Now then, Rachel, are there any boxes anywhere? We might need some.

Rachel No. Good point. I'll send Colin.

Howard Colin?

Rachel He'll be here a bit later.

Howard We didn't ask Colin to be part of this?

Rachel Part of what? He's bringing the Hoover.

Howard What?

Rachel The Hoover. Mum's doesn't suck properly so he's bringing mine.

Howard What for?

Rachel I've told you — hers doesn't suck.

Howard What?

Rachel Suck, Howard.

Howard I know, I know hers doesn't suck, Rachel, but I don't understand why we want a Hoover.

Rachel To give the place a going over. No one wants to view it in this condition. I wouldn't — put me right off. By the way, have you found out what it's worth yet, Howard?

Frances Look, can we discuss this later? We'll never get anywhere ——

Howard (*finally losing his patience*) Now hold on! Can I just say something before we start dismantling the place? In my view, this is a sensitive moment and there's really no need to behave like gannets.

Rachel Oh, Howard, what a thing to say.

Howard She was a remarkable woman. We owe her a lot.

Rachel No one's suggesting otherwise, are they? Come on, we said we wouldn't — let's not get all ——

Howard I'm not getting all anything, Rachel. I'm merely ... I'm merely saying it was a minor miracle she performed in this house, let's none of us forget it.

Frances Fine. We won't. Is that it? We've had a prayer and sermon; there's nothing else, is there?

Howard Apart from a little dignity, no.

Frances Dignity. Right. I'll be upstairs, if anyone needs me, labelling with pride.

Frances exits to the hall and goes up the stairs

Howard All heart, our sister.

Rachel She's all right. Needs a husband to soften her up. What about you?

Howard She's not my type. And I don't possess an ice-pick.

Rachel All right, I meant. Are you all right, Howard?

Howard Yes, yes.

Rachel You don't sound all right. You don't seem yourself at all.

Howard Really, I'm fine.

Rachel We're all going to miss her.

Howard It isn't that.

Rachel What, then?

Howard I just don't know how she did it, that's all, the three of us on her own like that.

Rachel Happens all the time, now.

Howard What, husbands drowning?

Rachel No, single parents, mothers being left.

Howard Now, it does, yes, but not then. Things were different then. D'you remember Uncle Nev, Rachel?

Rachel Uncle Nev: that's a name from the past. Whatever made you think of him?

Howard I'll tell you, I'll tell you what made me think of Uncle Nev, because it struck me with considerable force the other day what our mother actually achieved. What do you remember most about him?

Rachel Family friend, a good friend, picked up the pieces ... played cricket with you out there on the grass: an all-round ministering angel, if I'm not mistaken.

Howard Certainly that. Specifically, though?

Rachel Specifically? His lovely car with smelly seats.

Howard His car, yes, his black Austin. And where was he always taking us?

Rachel The hospital to visit Mum when Fran was ... born. Now, isn't that funny? I'd always thought in terms of our father dying *after* Fran arrived.

Howard Exactly. Me too. But he didn't — he was killed when our mother was still pregnant. We were so small we barely remember but the truth of it was she had to cope with all that with a baby inside her. She wasn't just a young widow — she was a pregnant young widow. Unbelievable. I wish I'd said something.

Rachel Uncle Nev ... whatever happened to him?

Howard The sheer strength of the woman; I don't know how she did it.

Rachel No. Well, as you say, she coped, didn't she?

Howard Mmmh?

Rachel She was a woman. First God made the world, then He made a man — and then He made a woman to cope with all the mess. You know what your trouble is?

Howard No, what's my trouble?

Rachel All those cars and bridges have made you think. You've come up here on your own from Bristol with all that time on the motorway to think.

Howard I'd better get on with this.

Rachel Where's Rosemary? I thought she'd be with you.

Howard Um ... she's away at the moment. Rather nice, this old desk, you know; we'll have to set a room aside for things like this.

Rachel Where?

Howard Next door should be safe enough.

Rachel No, Rosemary — where's she gone?

Howard Oh, not sure — the Lake District somewhere. She needed a break; with Toby at Edinburgh and Harriet in Bonn, she gets a bit down.

Rachel Why didn't you go with her? You like the Lakes.

Howard Not when she's got her brushes and canvas, I don't.

Rachel Oh, a painting holiday?

Howard Yes.

Rachel What, on her own, is she?

Howard A whole crowd of them, I gather, from this course she's been doing.

Rachel A course ... Well, she obviously takes it very seriously.

Howard Oh, frightfully. Though God knows why she had to choose one in London; she's been up and down like a yo-yo. Still, mine not to reason why ... It's no good — I'll have to fill up a couple of boxes and sort through it at home.

Rachel Gives her something to do, I expect.

Howard Mmmh? Oh, yes.

Rachel She must be quite good.

Howard Not bad. Brought home an excellent still life — well, I say excellent, not my cup of tea, frankly — a banana and a carving knife. But, there we are; you have to start somewhere. I said all the wrong things, of course. I asked her why the banana was bleeding; apparently, I'd missed the point altogether. Anyway, so long as she thinks she's achieving something.

Rachel Yes. Quite. Been gone long, has she?

Howard Lost track, to be honest.

Rachel Well, when's she coming back?

Howard Not sure. It's open-ended. I think I'll leave this now, 'til I get some boxes.

Rachel She rings, though?

Howard Who?

Rachel Rosemary — to see you're all right.

Howard Oh, yes, the odd call, you know.

Rachel Well. I'm sure, if she's with friends, it'll be doing her good.

Howard Oh, yes. Ha! Bit of an endurance test, apparently: they set off with eight and they're down to two.

Rachel Oh.

Howard The other six have downed easels and jacked it in.

Rachel Oh.

Howard So she said on the phone, anyway.

Rachel So, it's ... just her and one other, then.

Howard Her tutor chappie. Funny bloke — very young. Came to the house for a meal one evening. Odd-looking specimen.

Rachel And it's ... just her and him.

Howard The only two to stick it out.
Rachel On their own.
Howard Apparently.
Rachel Together.
Howard Boring the pants off each other and slicing their ears off. Ha! Good luck to them; not my idea of fun, I can tell you.

Frances comes downstairs briskly

Frances I was right. We will need boxes.
Rachel There's an off-licence next door; they'll have some.
Frances (*draining her teacup*) Ugh! That's better — it's full of dust up there. So, who's going to go? We can't wait for Colin.
Rachel Um ... Howard, could you? Then Fran and I can push on.
Howard Yes, all right. I'm going to need some for this desk, anyway. I'll ... er ... be back shortly.

Howard shuffles out through the front door

Frances He's going peculiar, that man. Is he always like that these days?
Rachel No. Something's going on.
Frances What d'you mean?
Rachel What I say. Listen ... come here a minute.
Frances What?
Rachel (*whispering*) Apparently ——
Frances Rachel, why are you whispering?
Rachel Because I don't want him to hear.
Frances He's gone. Do get on with it — what?
Rachel Apparently — and I may be quite wrong about this, but apparently — God, I hope I am, for Howard's sake — and anyway, I wouldn't have thought she was the type at all.
Frances Who?
Rachel Apparently, Rosemary ——
Frances Oh, I know what you're going to say.
Rachel What? How?
Frances Lawrence.
Rachel Who?
Frances This bloke she's buggered off with.
Rachel Lawrence?
Frances Yes.
Rachel It's true, then. How did you know? Has he told you?
Frances Who?
Rachel Howard.

Frances No.

Rachel No, he wouldn't. I don't think he knows himself. So, how did you know?

Frances About her and Lawrence?

Rachel Yes! And how did you know his name?

Frances Because I introduced them.

There is a pause. Rachel is dumbfounded

Not intentionally. She turned up at my flat one day with a full bladder and an armload of shopping. I had friends over and one of them was Lawrence. Well, don't look at me like that, it wasn't my fault!

Rachel He thinks she's on a painting course, Frances! With a proper teacher!

Frances She is. Lawrence is filling in as a City and Guilds tutor.

Rachel Huh! Filling in what, I ask myself. This is awful. How could you have let it happen?

Frances What was I supposed to do? Shout through the letter-box. Tell her to wet her knickers on the pavement because there are men in here?

Rachel God. Poor Howard. So, what now? What do we do?

Frances What d'you mean?

Rachel We must do something; we must tell him.

Frances Don't be so bloody silly.

Rachel What?

Frances It's a fling, Rachel, it happens. Lawrence is only a kid, anyway. She'll never keep up with him — I couldn't.

Rachel Oh, you're disgusting.

Frances Oh, so are you.

Rachel No, you are ... really ... you quite disgust me sometimes.

Frances She's racing the menopause, that's all. In a couple of weeks it'll all blow over; either her money'll give out or her back will. Howard'll find her on his doorstep pleading for a hot bath and an osteopath. I'm sure he knows, anyway.

Rachel Don't be daft; he hasn't a clue.

Frances Yes he does, he's just pretending.

Rachel Why?

Frances Convenience.

Rachel Frances, he doesn't even know where she is!

Frances Well, that makes three of us.

Rachel Liar. You've got his number, I'll bet.

Frances He's away, Rachel.

Rachel I know he's away! He's up in the Lakes with ... Oh, God, Frances! You're getting really hard in your old age, you know that?

Frances Life's hard. We all have to work our passage.

Rachel Well, it's time you stopped — give your passage a rest before you
catch something! God, I hope Mother isn't listening to this — she'd die.

The letter-box rattles

Colin (*off*) Rachel? ... Rachel?

Rachel and Frances both freeze; Rachel recovers first

Rachel It's all right, it's Colin ... Colin, don't do that.

Rachel opens the front door

> *Colin enters. He is in his mid-forties, wears a well-worn suit and carries
> a Hoover and a bag*

Colin Why? What have I done now? (*He comes into the living-room*)
Frances! You gorgeous creature! Look at this woman; loses ten years
whenever I see her.
Frances Hallo, Colin.
Colin So, what's your secret — jogging, is it? Ha! Where's Howard, then?
Rachel Getting boxes.
Colin Boxes, yes, I should say so. Bit of a job on here — what d'you reckon?
Still, she had a good innings. You can't complain if you've had a good ...

The front door opens noisily

> Ah, who's this?

> *Howard enters carrying several cardboard boxes which he deposits in the
> living-room during the following dialogue*

> Howard — morning.
Howard Oh, hallo Colin. Nice to see you.
Colin You, too. Family well? Rosemary not here, I see.
Howard No, she ... er ...
Colin I thought she looked blooming at the funeral — both said so, didn't
we, Rache? Been jogging as well, has she, or what?
Howard What?
Colin Rosemary. Like Fran, here — bought her a track suit and sent her round
the block? "And don't come back 'til you're ten years younger." Ha!
Frances (*heading for the hall*) Right. I'm off upstairs.
Colin (*moving to follow Frances*) Yes. Good idea.

Rachel (*stopping Colin*) Not you, Colin — there isn't room.

Colin What shall I do, then?

Rachel Make a start on the shed. You're good at sheds. Did you bring a change of clothes?

Colin Yep. Got the old boiler with me.

Rachel Well, get into it and get cracking. What about you, Howard; are you all right down here?

Howard Yes, fine. I'll push on with this desk.

Rachel Right. I'll see you later.

Rachel exits upstairs. Colin produces a boiler suit from his bag and steps into it as he chats to Howard

Colin Yes ... I've made my calls, my fitters are all out and there's not a yard of carpet in the warehouse that isn't spoken for. Good feeling, isn't it, Howard? Splashed out on a new van, did I tell you? Got a slogan down the side: "We like our clients — they walk all over us". Not bad, eh, what d'you reckon? No, I wasn't that convinced myself. Rachel's idea. So, how's your outfit? Must be running a tight ship if you can take the day off.

Howard Mmmh ... ? Oh, you know ...

Colin Don't turn your back for too long; no saying who's reaching for the cutlery while you're out the office.

Rachel appears upstairs and puts her head over the banisters

Rachel Colin?

Colin Yes, my love?

Rachel Shed.

Colin Right, my love. (*To Howard*) Shed.

Howard Right ... see you later.

Colin exits via the kitchen to the unseen shed. Rachel vanishes upstairs

Howard is alone with the bureau desk. He picks up a small pile of papers, gives them a cursory glance and drops them into a box on the floor. He opens a drawer and rummages about, pulling out another handful. Among the papers is a postcard which he looks at briefly before throwing it into a box with everything else. He is about to continue his work when he returns to the postcard, digging it out of the box and reading it closely. There is a pause. Suddenly, Howard begins urgently searching through the desk, pulling open drawers and grabbing at bundles of papers. He looks again at the postcard, studies it carefully and then puts it down. He looks vacantly out of the window for a moment, then turns on his heels and heads for the front door

Howard exits speedily through the front door, leaving it open

Colin enters from the kitchen with a Flymo hover mower

Colin Any thoughts on the Flymo, old man? ... Howard? ... (*He calls up the stairs*) Rachel?
Rachel (*off*) What?
Colin Is Howard up there?
Rachel (*off*) No!

Rachel's head appears over the banisters

I've got masses to do up here. What is it, Colin?
Colin I was looking for Howard. I wanted to ask him: if he's no use for this, and Fran hasn't, we could find a home for it, I reckon.
Rachel Fran won't want it. What would she want a Flymo for?
Colin Mowing flies? Ha!
Rachel Stop it. She might hear.

Howard returns at speed carrying a briefcase, nearly colliding with Colin and the Flymo

Colin Whoops!
Howard Sorry.
Colin My fault. Howard, I was wondering ...

Howard enters the living-room, followed by Colin and Rachel. Howard opens his briefcase and searches through it. He finds a letter and reads it during the following

This ... um ... this Flymo.
Rachel Everything all right, Howard?
Colin Seems a shame to just let it go and I was wondering ... (*He kneels on the floor fiddling with the mower*)
Rachel Howard, what are you doing?
Howard (*reading the letter*) Just a minute, Rachel.
Colin It's all snarled up at the bottom and I'm not even sure if she'll turn.
Howard (*finishing reading the letter*) Yes ... I thought so.
Rachel What is it? What have you found?
Howard Ask Frances to come down, would you?
Rachel She's up to her eyes, we both are: what is it?
Howard Rachel, just do as I ask, will you?
Rachel (*calling up the stairs*) Frances!

Frances (*off*) What?
Rachel (*going into the hall*) Howard wants you!

Frances appears at the top of the stairs

Frances What for?
Rachel I don't know.
Frances (*coming down the stairs*) I don't believe this!
Colin Anyway, worth having a bash, so what d'you think, Howard — if I can get her going?
Howard Mmmh?
Colin This Flymo.
Frances (*entering the living-room*) What is it now, Howard? We're never going to get anywhere if we keep ——
Howard (*handing her the postcard from the box*) Take a look at this.
Frances Good heavens, a postcard.
Rachel Plymouth, isn't it? (*She takes the postcard from Frances*) Yes. Look, Colin, that hotel we stayed in once. Two in the morning we all piled in when the camper sprung a leak.
Colin So it is. Wasn't a leak, though. The axle broke.
Rachel No, silly. The axle broke the year after, when the toilet flooded at Ely Cathedral.
Colin So it did.
Rachel And the cooker exploded. What's this all about, Howard?

Howard takes the card and hands it to Frances

Frances (*reading*) "Dearest Faith, Taken a few days break from the smoke. Thought of you a lot — reminds me of the old days ... blah-de-blah ... Love as always, D."
Rachel Dee who?
Frances The initial "D". Jolly fascinating, Howard — so what?
Rachel But who's it from, Fran?
Frances A man's writing, I'd guess: saucy old bag.
Rachel What, an admirer? At her age?
Frances Yes. Rather encouraging, don't you think? Thank you for showing me that, Howard, I feel a hundred times better. Now, I really must ——
Rachel Let's have a look. (*She takes the card from Frances*)
Howard (*taking the card from Rachel and giving it back to Frances again*) There's a PS down the side.

Frances turns the card on its side and reads. She has to hold it at arm's length to focus. Rachel also tries to read it but before she can make any headway, Frances drops her arm

Frances (*to Howard*) So?
Howard Doesn't that strike you as odd?
Frances No.
Howard (*handing her the letter he was reading*) Try this, then.
Rachel Who's that from?
Howard (*to Frances*) I got it last week and put it down to a clerical error.
Rachel What does it say?
Frances Just a minute, Rachel ...

Again Rachel tries to read over Frances's shoulder and again, before she can make any headway, Frances drops her arm and folds the letter

As you say: a clerical error.
Howard You don't see a connection?
Rachel Between what?
Frances I haven't the faintest idea what you're talking about, Howard.
Rachel Well, strangely enough, neither have I! Now, please, I'm forty-four and I want to see what's in these letters!

Frances hands Rachel the letter and postcard

Thank you. Been doing this since we were kids. I need my glasses. Where are they?
Frances Use mine. We're disintegrating at the same rate, I expect.
Rachel Now, let's see ...

Rachel reads the letter awkwardly through Frances' spectacles. There is a brooding silence between Howard and Frances

Colin (*surfacing from the Flymo*) What you got there, Rache?
Rachel Just a moment, Colin, I'm reading.
Colin Solicitors' letters: mumbo-jumbo, half the time. (*He returns to the Flymo*) Jammed solid this, you know ... something ... very wrong ... somewhere.
Rachel (*finishing the letter*) Right. Thank you. I don't understand a word of it.
Frances There's nothing to understand. The solicitor's pointing out that this house is still in their joint names — hers and our father's — and do we know of his whereabouts.
Rachel Well, that's absurd. He's at the bottom of Plymouth Sound, bless him; been there for forty years. We're not going to have trouble getting this house, are we?
Frances I doubt it, no.
Rachel What, then? And what's the significance of the postcard?

Frances None. It's from a friend thanking her for some photos she sent. Howard thinks there's a connection and I'm at a loss ... (*She moves to leave the room*) He's been doing Boris Karloff impressions since he got here and I'm fed up with it.

Rachel Well, hold on ... I can see one ... I can see a connection.

Frances (*from the doorway*) God. What?

Rachel Plymouth.

Frances What?

Rachel Apparently our father used to sail at Plymouth, he was drowned at Plymouth and this postcard's from Plymouth, so ... Plymouth.

Frances Plymouth.

Rachel Yes.

Frances Plymouth, Howard?

Colin We liked Plymouth, didn't we Rache? Found a terrific site. What was it called, now? Little something.

Howard Frances.

Frances Howard.

Howard Why would our mother send a complete stranger photographs of her family?

Frances Because he wasn't a complete stranger, she was his bit of fluff. Next question.

Howard Why would the deeds of this house still have our father's name on them?

Frances You tell me. No one bothered to take them off, I expect.

Howard Not true. It would have been done at probate after he died. (*He brandishes the postcard*) The sender signs himself "D", Fran.

Frances It's a bloody postcard, Howard!

Colin Titmoor! Little Titmoor — that was it. Wonderful view. Twenty miles in all directions.

Rachel Would someone mind telling me what you're talking about?

Colin Yes, I was trying to remember ——

Rachel Not you, Colin.

Frances He's talking rubbish.

Howard There's one way to find out, isn't there? (*He goes into the hall*) Contact him.

Rachel (*following Howard*) Contact who?

Frances And, how d'you propose to do that? The phone book?

Howard Certainly ... (*He reaches beneath the telephone table and starts chucking directories about*) ... if there's nothing in her address book. Have a look, Rachel, see if you can find it.

Rachel (*to Frances*) Find what? Who's he talking about? (*To Howard in the hall*) Look, I'm sorry to be thick about this, but I'm still in Plymouth!

Colin Spanner, that's what I need. Shan't be long.

Colin exits through the front door

Rachel returns to Frances in the living-room

Rachel Well?
Frances Howard is trying to suggest that our father who art in heaven, isn't.
Rachel What?
Frances Howard thinks he's still alive. He thinks the postcard says so.
Rachel Oh, don't be so stupid!

Howard returns to the living-room with the phone book and begins hunting through it

Howard, don't be so stupid! What are you thinking of?
Howard A sailing accident, body never found, "Sorry children — no grave — nothing to put your flowers on." You must admit it was very convenient.
Rachel For who? Howard, I don't like this, it's making me feel peculiar.
Frances Just ignore him.
Rachel You remember it happening, we both do. One of our earliest memories, we always said — crying her eyes out over the sink.
Howard Lots of things make people cry, Rachel. Lots of ways to lose a husband.
Rachel What d'you mean?
Howard They can walk out, disappear.
Rachel But there's the police and files. People have to be told. This isn't *Dallas*, you know. People don't step in and out of showers when it suits them.
Howard Not when a husband does a bunk. No one has to be told anything — except the children, and told we were.
Rachel That he'd drowned.
Howard Exactly. When he could have been walking about, same name, same everything. (*He finds what he's been looking for in the directory*) Templeton D. — here we are. Not many of them, either.
Rachel Oh, this is macabre. Stop it, Howard. Stop him, Fran.
Howard Look, it's a puzzle. At this stage, that's all I'm saying.
Rachel But he'd have surfaced somewhere before now. He'd have surfaced, Howard.
Howard He just has — on the deeds of the house. If he'd ever been declared officially dead, there's no way his name would have stayed on them and, if he was still breathing, there's no way his name could have been taken off. So.
Rachel So what? She made it all up?
Howard I don't know.

Rachel Is that what you're saying?

Howard Rachel, I don't know!

Rachel Why? Why would she lie to us for all those years? Telling her own children that their father's dead when he isn't? That's a terrible thing for a mother to do and even worse of you to suggest it. Tell him, Frances.

Frances Howard, you're upsetting Rachel and I want to get on. If you're so obsessed with it, go to the Public Records Office or something and find his bloody death certificate. In the meantime, stop wasting everyone's ——

Howard pushes past the others, goes into the hall and picks up the phone

What are you doing? (*She realizes what he is up to*) Oh, don't be absurd. You're not going to suddenly find him on the end of a phone.

Howard You're right. Not this one, anyway, they've cut it off. I'll get mine from the car.

Frances Come on, Rachel.

Brushing past Colin and the Flymo, Howard exits through the front door

Colin Whoops!

Howard (*off*) Sorry!

Colin My fault. I've done it, by the ... (*To Rachel*) Look at that. I've done it, I reckon.

Rachel Mmmh? Oh, good. Well done, Colin.

Colin Look at that. (*He shows her the underside of the Flymo*) Wrapped right round the inner spindle.

Rachel Was it. Was it, really.

Frances Rachel, are you coming or what?

Rachel Right ... yes.

Frances heads up the stairs

Rachel peers through the front door

Frances Rachel — come on!

Frances exits. Howard marches back in with his portable phone

Frances (*off*) Rachel! For the last time!

Rachel Right. Yes. I'm coming, Frances.

Rachel goes upstairs, peering over the banisters; then she exits

Howard refers to the phone book and dials

Colin So, what d'you reckon about this Flymo?
Howard Mmmh?
Colin I think she'll run now and there's a young couple next door, living off
baked beans and a lot of enthusiasm, be pretty pleased to get their hands
on this. What d'you think?
Howard Engaged, engaged ...
Colin No, married: everything above board.
Howard (*looking at the phone book and re-dialling*) Sorry, Colin — what?
Colin You've no objection, then?
Howard To what? Yes, take it by all means. (*Into the phone*) Hallo, yes. I'm
sorry to trouble you.
Colin Right. I'll go and give her a try, then.

Colin exits into the kitchen with the Flymo, heading for the garden

Howard (*into the phone*) I'm not sure if I've got the right number but ... is
there a Mr David Templeton living there?

Rachel's head appears over the banisters

David, yes. ... I see. Sorry to have bothered you. (*He hangs up*)

Howard dials another number. He darts a look at Rachel

Rachel vanishes

*Howard is about to speak on the phone when the Flymo starts up in the
garden at close quarters*

Howard Colin! (*He leans out of the window*) Colin! I can't hear!
Colin (*off*) I know! Marvellous! Running a treat!
Howard I can't hear! I'm on the phone!
Colin (*off*) Sorry! Sorry!

The sound of the Flymo dies

Howard (*into the phone*) Yes. This is a message for a Mr David Templeton.
I don't know if it's the right number but if someone of that name does live
there, could he please ring me? My mobile number is o-eight-three-one-
three-three-six-three-two-one. Thank you very much. (*He hangs up and
returns to the phone book*)

Colin enters

Colin Sorry about that. Going perfectly, now.
Howard Splendid. I couldn't hear, that's all.
Colin (*toying with the phone*) Pretty flashy instrument, this.
Howard Mmmh? Yes. It's a phone.
Colin Could do with one of these, myself. Use it any place, can you?
Howard More or less. (*He takes the phone and re-dials*)

Frances and Rachel come downstairs with full bin-liners

Colin exits through the kitchen

Rachel It is possible, though.
Frances It's rubbish. I'm telling you, Rachel, he's completely off his trolley.
Rachel What, because of Rosemary, you mean? Is he having a breakdown?
Frances Wouldn't you?

Howard, clearly getting bad reception on the phone, manoeuvres oddly about the room for the optimum position. Rachel and Frances peer at him from the hall

Rachel All right, Howard?
Howard One wrong number, one answer-machine and one engaged, so far — which is still engaged. (*He hangs up the phone and returns to the directory*)
Frances Why London, anyway?
Howard "A break from the smoke", the postcard said.

The phone rings. No-one moves

Howard I left a message on a machine just now.
Frances Well, aren't you going to answer it?
Howard A Highbury number. I said to ring back if someone of that name lived there.

Colin enters from the kitchen with an assortment of garden tools

Colin Garden shears and a strimmer: any takers? No? Phone's ringing, by the way.

Colin exits

Frances (*grabbing the phone*) I'm not putting up with this ... (*Into the phone*) Sorry to have troubled you — wrong num—— Yes. Who is this? ... God.

Sorry. I didn't recognize ... No, no. He's just here. Hold on. ... (*She hands the phone to Howard*) For you. Rosemary.

Howard Rosemary?

Frances Your wife ... Well, take it.

Howard (*into the phone*) Rosemary, hallo darling — how lovely ...

During the following speech there is a pantomime of gesturing: Frances tells Rachel to come away upstairs; Rachel tells Frances to go on ahead; Howard tells both of them there's no need to leave the room

Eventually Frances exits upstairs

Rachel hovers in the hall

No, no. A little surprised, that's all; I was expecting someone else. ... Oh, nothing. No-one. ... No, I'm at Mother's with Rachel and Frances, clearing up. Where are you? ... Oh, really? Whereabouts? ... Oh. ... Well, not really, sweetheart, can't it wait? ... Yes, but, if you're in London you're on your way home, presumably; we can talk then, can't we? ... No, I'm not being difficult, darling; we're all here, everyone's busy. ... Rosemary? (*He hangs up*)

Rachel (*appearing from the shadows of the hall. Breezily*) All well?

Howard Yes, fine. Got cut off, I think.

Rachel Oh dear. Where was she?

Howard Didn't say — London somewhere.

Rachel London? I thought she was in the Lakes with ... the Lakes.

Howard Well, she isn't. She's in London with the traffic.

Rachel Right ... What was she ringing about, then?

Howard Oh, she wanted to meet and chat or something. Now, pipe down, I'm trying to concentrate.

Rachel Howard, don't you think you should?

Howard What?

Rachel Meet. It might be important.

Howard I doubt it. If it is, she can come over here, can't she? (*He dials again*)

Rachel What are you doing?

Howard Trying this number again; it's been engaged so far.

Rachel But if you were cut off, she's probably trying to ring you back, isn't she?

Howard Probably.

Frances comes down the stairs and enters the living-room

Rachel (*taking the phone from him*) Put that thing down, Howard, and listen to me!

Howard Rachel, whatever's got into you?

Rachel Your wife has just telephoned you. The least you can do is ring her back.

Frances Don't interfere, Rachel.

Howard I would but unfortunately I don't have a number.

Rachel London, she said, didn't she?

Howard Yes?

Rachel Well, they're obviously at his flat, aren't they?

Howard Whose flat?

Rachel Lawrence's flat. Fran'll have ... (*She claps her hand over her mouth*)

Frances Oh, well done Rachel, nice one.

Howard What will Fran have?

Rachel Look, Howard, it wasn't her fault.

Howard What wasn't?

Frances Shut up and throw me my bag, will you?

Rachel passes Frances her bag. Frances digs into it, pulls out an address book and starts leafing through it

Howard Would someone mind telling me what's going on?

Rachel It was an accident. She turned up at Frances' flat wanting to spend a penny.

Howard Who did?

Rachel Rosemary. It wasn't Fran's fault.

Howard And she had an accident. What are you talking about?

Frances (*finding a name in her address book*) Prescott, here we are. Lawrence Prescott.

Howard Lawrence Prescott? Why do I know that name? Look, what the hell's going on here?

Frances (*writing the number on the top sheet of the notepad*) Stop playing games, Howard. (*She tears it off and hands it to Howard*) There's the number, if you want to ring her. Now, let's get back to work, shall we?

Howard Wait a minute, this is the painter boy who's been teaching her, isn't it? How come you've got his phone number?

Frances He's a friend of mine.

Howard Good grief. What a coincidence. You've not been doing this painting thing as well, have you?

Frances God.

Howard What makes you think I'll find Rosemary there, anyway?

Frances Howard, this is silly. We know.

Howard Know what?

There is a pause

Frances OK. Have it your own way. You've got the number, you know where she is — my hands are clean.

Howard Hold on, hold on. She came to your flat, and that's where she met him; so, you think ...

Frances Yes, and so do you. In fact none of us "think", we all "know".

Howard Oh, don't be ridiculous!

Frances Howard, I'm not playing this game.

Howard He's a kid — he's Toby's age!

Frances So?

Howard She's far too old. Women of that age don't ...

Frances Women of our age don't what?

Howard You know what I mean. What could he possibly see in her?

Frances I can't imagine, but clearly he does and the way to be sure is to ring the number and see.

Howard (*screwing up the piece of paper and throwing it on the floor*) I'll do nothing of the sort.

Frances No, of course you won't. Because if you do and she answers — which she will — you'll be obliged to do something, won't you?

The phone rings

Whoops! There we are, she's made it easy for you. All you have to do now is ask her.

Colin enters from the kitchen laden with seed boxes and pot plants

Colin You know the Hubbards, Rachel, the two old dears in the alms-houses; I reckon they'd like all these ... Rachel? Don't tell me that phone's still ringing!

Rachel Go on, Howard, answer it.

Howard No.

Frances Well, I'm not picking it up.

Rachel Neither am I.

Colin I'll have a turn, then, I don't mind ... (*Into the phone*) Hallo Norway! May we have your votes please? ... Sorry? ... Hold on a minute. (*To the others*) David Templeton — someone left a message for him.

Frances God, I can't bear it.

Howard (*taking the phone; into it*) Hallo?

Colin I'll put these in the back of the car, Rache. Shan't be long.

Colin struggles off with his seed boxes

Howard (*into the phone*) David Templeton — yes, that's right. Who am I speaking to, please? ... Well, could I have a word with him? ... Rather urgent, yes ... No, he won't know me but ... No, I'd rather speak to him myself ... If you wouldn't mind, and I'll hang on ... (*To Rachel and Frances*) She's gone to get him. He's up a ladder or something. Apparently, that was his wife.

Rachel His wife? Oh well. There we are, then; it's obviously not him.

Howard Unless he's a bigamist.

Rachel Don't be so silly.

Frances Or a Mormon.

Rachel Stop it, Fran. We're Church of England in our family, always have been.

Frances Howard, will you please ring off?

Howard I can't ring off. He's fixing the roof. She's gone all the way out to drag him in.

Frances (*reaching for the phone*) Come on. Give it to me.

Howard No.

Frances (*snatching the phone*) Howard!

Howard What the hell d'you think you're doing?

Frances Highbury you said, didn't you?

Howard Yes. Give that back, Frances!

Frances Our father doesn't live in Highbury, Howard. He lives in Parsons Green ... (*she pauses*) ... and what's more, he's ex-directory. (*She hands Howard the phone*)

Howard (*suddenly hearing a voice on the phone*) Sorry. Wrong number. (*He hangs up*) I don't believe you.

Frances You'd have found out soon enough.

Howard Meaning what?

Frances In his own time. He's writing to us.

Rachel You mean it's true?

Frances Yes. But this isn't how he wanted it.

Howard Oh. Really?

Frances Look. He read about Mother's death in the papers and thought it was time he got in touch.

Howard Yes. Well, it has been a while.

Frances She'd always refused to give him our addresses so he did exactly what you've been doing except he drew a blank with you because he didn't know you lived in Bristol and he drew a blank with Rachel because he didn't know her married name. He did, however, get hold of me.

Rachel I don't believe you. She's playing games, Howard.

Frances I'm not, actually.

Rachel How long have you known, then?

Frances Not long. I got a phone call and then a letter. I haven't met him or anything. I know little more than you.

Howard Ha! Only that he's alive, that's all!

Rachel Show me.

Frances What?

Rachel The letter, come on.

Frances I haven't got it here; don't be daft.

Rachel You're lying — she's lying, Howard.

Howard I don't think she is, Rachel. All that carry-on with phone calls — why in God's name didn't you say something?

Frances Because I thought you'd drop it.

Howard He's our father, Frances!

Frances Drop it for now, I meant, and let him do it his own way — write his letters, meet with the three of us and talk sensibly. I said I would.

Rachel I can't take this in at all.

Howard Where does he live, you say?

Frances Parsons Green.

Howard But ... that's ten minutes from here — down the road, virtually.

Frances Virtually.

Howard What, all these years? Has he always lived there?

Frances I don't know.

Howard What, down the bloody road?

Frances I don't know! I don't know! You'll have to ask him yourself, won't you?

Howard I will. We will. Too bloody right. Let's get him here. What's his address?

Frances No, Howard. I really ——

Howard Listen, Frances, I've just about had it up to here with you. Now, have you got his address and phone number or not?

Frances Both. Yes.

Howard Give them to me, then.

Frances Howard ...

Howard picks up Frances' bag and empties the contents all over the sofa

OK ... OK ... (*She opens her address book*) There — Templeton D.

Rachel Sitting there ... all the bloody time. What else is in that? You haven't got Tricia's GCSE results, have you?

Howard (*picking up the phone to dial, then hesitating*) On second thoughts, you ring him — he's spoken to you.

Frances That's not fair. He'll think I told you.

Howard (*handing Frances the phone*) Hold this. Press that. Dial ...

Frances heads for the kitchen door with the phone

Where are you going?

Frances Away from you — I'm not doing this with you two listening.

Frances exits to the kitchen

Rachel hovers by the kitchen door

Howard Come away, Rachel. Let her get on with it.
Rachel I don't trust her. I've never trusted her.
Howard Down the bloody road. Where's he been, this man? Where the hell's he been?
Rachel She tried to tell me you were having a breakdown! I need a brandy. We all do. Where's Colin? (*She calls*) Colin?

Colin enters through the front door

Colin I've loaded them up, Rache. Now what about ...?
Rachel Never mind all that. There's an off-licence next door — go and get a bottle of brandy.
Colin Brandy? You don't drink brandy.
Rachel I am today. What else, Howard?
Colin Is somebody sick?
Rachel A bottle of wine — no, sherry — he'll like a drop of sherry, I expect.
Colin Who will?
Rachel (*steering Colin to the front door*) A decent bottle of medium dry, Colin, and some nibbles as well.
Colin Oh, a party? Are we having a party?
Rachel No we're not having a party, Colin. (*She pushes Colin out of the door*) Just GO!

Colin exits

Rachel slams the front door and hurries back into the living-room

Rachel Now then ... This room needs straightening up.
Howard She was pregnant. How could he have done it?
Rachel Out of the way, Howard, please.

Frances enters casually

Frances (*pondering the phone*) How d'you switch this thing off?

Howard tries to take the phone from Frances. She snatches it away and then hands it to him slowly and in her own time. He clicks it off. Frances returns her address book to her bag and looks up at the other two watching her

It's all right — he's coming.

Howard When?

Frances Now. He's on his way.

Rachel Oh my God ... Glasses, we'll need some glasses, Fran, and look at the state of this place. Come on, Howard, shift yourself and let's get a bit of order ...

Rachel pushes Howard and plumps the cushions on the sofa and chairs

Howard How — driving?

Rachel (*pushing past Howard, heading for the kitchen*) Excuse me.

Rachel exits into the kitchen

Frances Yes. About ten minutes, he reckoned.

Howard Let's hope he's careful. Huh. Be ironic, that would — after forty years, he wraps himself round some traffic lights.

Rachel enters with a can of spray polish and a duster

Howard He really is coming?

Frances I just told you, didn't I?

Rachel attacks surfaces with the polish and duster

Howard Rachel, what are you doing?

Rachel What does it look like? (*She abandons the polishing and unravels the Hoover flex*) Mind yourselves, you two — I want to plug this in ...

Frances Rachel ...

Rachel Glasses, Fran — come on. There's some in the kitchen but they'll need a good wash. Just mind, will you Howard? And get this lot off the floor ... (*She switches the Hoover on and attacks the carpet*) Frances! Don't just stand there — make yourself useful for once! Run upstairs, Howard, and make sure there's paper in the toilet.

Howard and Frances watch Rachel for a moment, mesmerized

Howard Rachel!

Frances Rachel!

Rachel hoovers on like someone possessed. Howard pulls the plug from the wall. There is a silence

Howard What on earth d'you think you're doing?

Rachel stares blankly at the Hoover and then at them

Rachel I don't know ... I don't know what I'm doing. (*She breaks down silently*)

Howard puts an arm round Rachel. Frances wanders off, slightly irritated

Howard Come on.
Rachel (*struggling with a hanky*) Oh ... stupid. I'll be all right in a minute. Ha! Look at me — I'm sweating, I'm crying, I'm completely evaporating ... "This is Howard, that's Frances and the puddle on the floor was Rachel." I wonder what he looks like. I wonder what we look like? It's been forty years — he'll see quite a difference, I expect. Oh shut up, Rachel. Just shut up!
Frances What happens about this house, Howard?
Howard Mmmh? Oh, God knows. Half his probably — if it's in their ... (*suddenly realizing*) ... joint names. Of course. He must have waited for this for a long time.
Frances He'll have paid for it originally. He's entitled to it.
Howard Ha! He's what?
Frances Come on. Probably his only asset.
Howard Probably why he's come up for air. Anyway, let's not get side-tracked into that.

The letter box rattles. They all freeze

Howard Bit quick, wasn't it?
Frances Shall I go or will you?
Rachel Well, someone go: we're not waiting another forty years.

Frances and Rachel brace themselves; Howard checks his tie and sets off towards the front door

Rachel Howard! Wait! (*She bundles up the Hoover flex*)
Howard Ready now?
Rachel Almost. (*She pushes the Hoover into a corner*)
Howard Come on, Rachel.
Rachel (*straightening her frock and composing herself*) Right. Ready.

Howard goes to the front door, takes a deep breath and opens it

Colin strides in

No-one moves during the following dialogue

Colin Sorry, I left without a bean on me. Felt a right prat — all that booze laid out on the counter and ... (*He finds his jacket*) Wallet. Right. Sorry about that; try again.

Colin exits

Howard pushes the door shut

The door opens again and Colin sticks his head round it

Leave it on the latch, I should.

Colin exits

Howard closes the door and returns to the living-room

Rachel I don't think I can take much more of this.
Frances I wonder what it'll actually fetch, though.
Rachel Oh, what does it matter, Fran? First things first, that's what I say. Anyway, it can't be much: ours is twice this size and Colin paid ... what, forty thousand?
Frances When?
Rachel Ten years ago — no, twelve.
Frances Exactly. We've had a boom since then.
Rachel And a slump ... and look at the state of it.
Frances You must have some idea what the agent said, Howard.
Howard God ... Two, I think — I don't know — I seem to remember the figure two.
Frances Two what?
Howard Two hundred.
Rachel Ha! Two hundred pounds? Don't be ridiculous.
Howard Two hundred thousand, Rachel — don't you be ridiculous. Now, let's keep money well out of this, shall we? The last thing we want is to haggle over cash.

There is a brief pause. Rachel acquires the look of someone who has unexpectedly arrived on another planet

Rachel Two hundred thousand pounds? Howard, you're joking.
Howard No, Rachel, I seem to remember that's what he said; or one-eighty if the survey's bad.
Rachel One-eighty? For this heap?
Howard It's not a heap, it's the house we grew up in.
Rachel Sod the survey, I'll settle for a hundred and fifty. Howard, are you

sure you've got this right? I mean, I thought sixty at the most, twenty each. If it's two hundred, you're talking ... well, that's ——

Frances Seventy each — or thereabouts.

Rachel It is. You're right.

Howard It's not the point, Rachel — and anyway, it's not, it's a hundred between the three of us.

Rachel Why? How d'you make that out?

Howard He gets half.

Rachel Who does?

Frances He does.

Rachel So we get, what, thirty-five each? Well, that's not very fair, is it? Is it, Howard? He gets a hundred and we get thirty-five; I don't call that very fair, do you?

Howard It's still more than you were expecting.

Rachel Even so.

Howard Rachel, it's the law.

Rachel But — after forty years, he can't just march in here and ... and ...

Frances Collect.

Rachel Yes! No. I'm sure it's not as crude as that, Fran. Look, what are we saying? He's our father, for goodness sake. I'm sure, when it comes to it ——

Howard (*exploding*) For the last time, the money isn't the issue here!

Rachel No one's saying it, Howard! Of course money isn't the issue here! I'm discussing a principle, that's all. It wouldn't be right, it would be quite wrong if ... Seventy thousand — solve all our problems, that would.

The letter box rattles. There is a brief pause

Colin (*through the letter box*) Me again!

Rachel Oh, Colin ... I wish he wouldn't keep doing that ... (*She opens the door to him*)

Colin enters carrying a bag containing brandy and sherry bottles, nibbles etc.

I wish you wouldn't keep doing that, Colin.

Colin I said to leave it on the latch. I got some, anyway.

Rachel Good. Let's get it open.

Colin Friendly round here, aren't they? Funny old geezer started waving at me.

Rachel Where?

Colin Parking his car.

Rachel My God, he's here.

Howard Right.

Rachel He's here, Howard!

Howard I know!

Colin Who's here? Who are you expecting?

Rachel Where's that brandy, Colin? I need a drink before I do this.

Colin Do what? Would someone mind telling me what's going on?

Rachel Glasses; where are they, Fran?

Frances In the kitchen. I'll go, you answer the door, Howard. (*She heads into the kitchen*)

Howard (*following Frances*) No, I'll go — you answer the door.

Frances and Howard exit into the kitchen

Rachel, left alone, takes a swig from the brandy bottle. The doorbell rings (the first time we've heard it). Rachel freezes with a mouthful of brandy. She gulps it down, takes two steps to the front door and, as if with her throat ablaze, gestures to Colin to go instead

Rachel turns tail and exits to the kitchen

Colin saunters to the front door and opens it

Colin Ah ... Hallo again.

CURTAIN

ACT II

The same

The action begins exactly where Act I left off. Colin stands by the open front door, outside which stands David, a distinguished-looking gentleman with an ageless quality which could put him anywhere between sixty and seventy years old

Colin Sorry I rushed off earlier.
David No, no, that's quite all right.
Colin I had a bag full of booze about to collapse on me. Come in.
David Thank you.
Colin So — we meet again.
David Yes. Been a long time.
Colin Ha! Yes. You were lucky to find a meter; you can drive round for hours and ... something wrong?
David Photographs can be deceptive.
Colin What photographs? Look, let's find the other three.
David Other three?
Colin There's four of us here ... (*He calls*) Rachel!

Colin leads David into the living-room

There is a slight kerfuffle with the kitchen door and then Howard opens it firmly and enters, followed by Frances

Howard Ah, there you are. We were just ... I'm Howard.
David Yes. I realize that now ... Hallo, Howard.
Howard And this is Frances.
David Frances.
Howard And Rachel. Where's Rachel? She was here a minute ago.
Colin Rachel?

Rachel enters, still clutching the brandy bottle. She has, faintly, the air of a ten-year-old

Howard Yes, here we are: this is Rachel.
David Hallo, Rachel.

Rachel Hallo.
Howard Well.
David Well.
Colin Shall we have a drink, then?
David Not for me, I'm driving.
Colin I'm Colin, by the way.
David Colin ... Oh, right, Rachel's husband.
Colin Yes! How did you know?
David I saw a picture, once. Congratulations.
Colin Thanks very ... what for?
David Marrying Rachel.
Colin Oh, it was ... Look, I'm sorry but who are you? I don't know who you are at all.
David Hasn't Rachel told you?
Colin No.

There is a pause

Sorry to press the point but ...
Howard He's your father-in-law, Colin.
Colin He's what — sorry?
Rachel My ... our father.
Colin (*chuckling, embarrassed, as if having difficulty taking this in*) Really? But I thought ... Well, what a turn-up. Shouldn't we be celebrating or something?
Howard Why don't we all sit down?
Colin Yes, good idea.
Rachel Glasses. Organize some glasses, Colin, would you? In the kitchen.
Colin Glasses. Right.

Colin exits

The others sit. David finds himself with the wing chair

David (*moving the newspaper and pen*) Someone else likes doing the crossword too, I see.
Howard It was Mother's. Nothing's been touched. You'll see from the date.
David (*carefully putting the newspaper to one side*) Look. I don't quite know how to begin this, so can I ——

Colin puts his head round the kitchen door

Colin These glasses, Rache: where, exactly?

Rachel The cupboard above the sink.
Colin Right.
Rachel There's a set of six.
Colin Right.
Rachel So, be careful.
Colin Right.

Colin disappears

Rachel He has a way with glasses. Sorry.
David Can I simply say two things. Firstly, there's a lot of ground to cover and there's no point in trying to do it all in one go, so let's just regard this initial gathering as ... an ice-breaker. How does that sound?

The sounds of a glass smashing and Colin cursing come from the the kitchen

Secondly, shall we just agree for you to call me David. It saves any awkwardness.

Colin enters with a tray of glasses

Here we are, Pa! Glasses for the charging of ... it's a set of five now, I'm afraid, but that's all right because there's only five of us. Ha!
David Really — nothing for me.
Colin Four, then; I can go and smash another.

Colin pours sherry and hands out glasses

Rachel Would you like some tea or coffee?
David I'm fine.
Colin Should be champagne, really, toast you properly ... This is a first for me; resurrections don't run in my family. Ha! Wonderful; our own little Easter. Well, cheers. Welcome home. (*He drinks*) Mmmh. Not a bad drop of grape, that.
Rachel Colin, I think ——
Colin So, where've you been? What's the story? Shame about the timing — the old girl will be sorry to have missed you.
Howard Colin, I hope you won't think me rude but this is a family matter and somewhat delicate. Would you mind terribly just leaving us for a while?
Colin Oh. Yes. All right — but I am Rachel's husband.
Howard Indeed you are. No offence meant.
Colin OK ... I'll ... um ... carry on in the shed.

Colin shuffles off through the kitchen

Rachel I'll talk to him later.

David This is a strange experience, perhaps more so for me than it is for you.

Howard Oh, I don't know. It's not every day we unearth a parent.

David No. Quite. But you're faced with one stranger and I'm faced with three.

Howard At least you knew we were alive.

Frances We're here, together, in the same room, Howard. That's more than enough to be going on with.

Rachel I'm glad you met Colin.

David He seemed very nice, Rachel. You've chosen well.

Rachel Oh, I don't know about that ... Well, what I mean is he did the choosing, all those years ago.

David The pictures I've seen of the children, they look marvellous.

Rachel They are. Colin's so good with them, too. Always there when he's need —— We've got a camper, you know, take it everywhere. All five of us, all tucked up. D'you get away much, David?

David Not much. I live alone, and, at my age ——

Frances Yes, what is your age, if it's not a rude question? We were trying to work it out.

David Not at all: sixty-nine.

Howard Sixty-nine? But she was over eighty.

David Yes, I imagine she was.

Howard All those years between you?

Frances D'you find that strange, Howard?

Howard A little. Don't you? No, of course, stupid of me.

David They were strange times. There'd been a war, the place was a shambles ...

Howard So you all rushed out and married your mothers. That's understandable.

Frances Howard.

Rachel How did you and she meet?

David I was finishing my National Service and volunteered for bombs.

Rachel Bombs?

Howard What kind of bombs?

David The exploding kind. Disposing of them, principally. The place was still littered with them in those days.

Howard And you were what age at this point?

David Twenty-two.

Howard Which would have made her ...?

David Thirty-four.

Howard Right. I just wanted to get the picture clear. So, there you were —

a fully qualified bomb chap sporting his first pair of long trousers — then what?

David I was called out to her street. It was a fairly simple job, as these things went — until your mother brought me a cup of tea. Ha! Nearly blew us all to Kingdom come.

Howard Saved a lot of angst all round, wouldn't it?

Frances Howard, shut up.

David No, it's all right, my dear. I didn't expect this to be easy.

Rachel What an odd thought: all our lives — mine, Frances, Howard, his two, my three — all resting in the skill of your fingers.

Howard No, I'm sorry. I can't take any more of this.

Rachel More of what?

Howard The point is — he walked out.

Rachel How d'you know? We haven't got to that bit, yet.

Howard For God's sake, Rachel. I'll tell you what happened next. A cup of tea led to a call of nature and a call of nature, as you've already pointed out once today, can produce spectacular results. She got pregnant — with me — so he did the honourable thing and married her. They then had you, Rachel, and then got cracking on Frances. By which time she was — let's see — thirty-seven — no, eight — and he was twenty-six. He got bored and pushed off leaving Mother with us two and Fran in the oven. Am I right? *(He pauses)* My God. I am.

David I loved your mother very much.

Howard But you found someone else. Something with a little less mileage on the clock.

Frances Howard, I think that's enough.

Howard Mind you, on one level, who could blame him? There she is pushing middle age, what kid in his right mind's going to want to know?

David Look, it's perfectly true: I behaved very foolishly with another woman, but ...

Howard Yes, yes, smacked wrists and ten "Hail Marys", but that's not the point, is it?

Rachel To leave your wife when she's pregnant ...

David I didn't know she was pregnant, Rachel, and, to the best of my knowledge, neither did she — not at that stage.

Howard But that's not the point, either, is it?

Frances What is the point then, Howard?

Howard What the hell was he doing knocking around with an older woman — our mother — to begin with?

Frances Ah. Yes. I should have guessed.

Rachel I don't know what you're complaining about, Howard, because if he hadn't, you wouldn't even be here — none of us would.

Howard What was it, a mother fixation or something?

Frances Oh for God's sake, Howard, it happens! Just accept it.

Howard Gets her pregnant three times and pushes off. No husband to look after her and, at her age, no prospect of a replacement. Unbelievable.

David She didn't need a replacement, Howard.

Frances Of course she didn't. She could manage perfectly well without.

David No she couldn't, Frances — but she had me.

Frances I thought you legged it.

David I came back after a couple of months ... but she wouldn't let me in.

Frances Ha! Good for her.

David I did everything in my power to persuade her, of course — especially when I saw her condition — but she was adamant.

Rachel She needed you. So did we.

David Well obviously, Rachel, and that's what I told her. "The aftermath of war," she said. There were "Fatherless children everywhere so three more wouldn't make a difference ... Better a dead father than an unloving one." She forbade me ever to come near you again.

Howard And here you are.

David Yes.

Rachel But you wrote to each other. Howard found a card.

David Yes. Out of the blue, she wrote and told me that an old and mutual friend had died: Neville Williams, you may remember him.

Rachel Ah, Uncle Nev, we were talking about him earlier, weren't we, Howard? Thought the world of Uncle Nev, Howard did; like a father to him ... Well ... anyway, what happened to him?

David Went abroad, found himself a wife, became a wealthy man, by all accounts. Died about ten years ago. Anyway, we did begin a correspondence — she sent photos and so forth — but it was all much later.

Howard And you never re-married.

David No.

Howard So what've you been doing with yourself?

David I became a senior consultant to an engineering firm in Wales, then retired and moved back to London.

Howard Parsons Green.

David Yes. I have my books, my boat and a cottage in Devon to escape to.

Howard Plymouth.

David Yes.

Howard How very pleasant.

Rachel Look, we're all here, aren't we? That's the main thing, surely.

Howard We're not, as a matter of fact.

Frances She's gone, Howard. We can't change that. And we all survived.

Howard Lucky us.

Rachel Well, I think so. A lot of people have a lot worse. I think we should just be practical ... I mean, there's a lot we need to sort out, isn't there? Lots of things to ... well ... you know — iron out.

There is a pause

David This room, it's hardly changed, you know. Most odd being in it again.
Rachel We've made a start on sorting through.
David Have you. Yes. That desk over there: a gift, that was, from my great aunt.
Rachel Oh, you must have it. The others won't mind, I'm sure — and any other bits and pieces, you know, of sentimental value, you just say. Perhaps you'd like to have a wander round and see if there's anything else before we ... well ... before it's too late.
David A wander round. I'd like that.
Rachel (*putting her arm through David's*) Come along, then. Anyone else?
Frances (*looking at her watch*) Yes, all right but ...
Rachel Paris — for the weekend. Flies everywhere, this one. Never stops. Spends half her life with her legs in the air. Howard, are you with us?
Howard I'll skip the tour if you don't mind.

Rachel, Frances and David go into the hall

David I wallpapered this hall, you know.
Rachel Did you, really? Had a lick or two of paint since then. You did a good job — didn't he? A good job on this hall, Fran?
David Notice anything odd about it?
Rachel No.
David The pattern. Upside down.
Rachel Ha! So it is. All those years and we never noticed. See that, Fran — upside down? Up we go, then ... (*She heads up the stairs*) We always say, Colin and I, we always say: any couple thinking of marriage should paper a room together first. The acid test, we always say ...

Rachel, Frances and David disappear upstairs

Howard strolls over to Frances' bag, digs around in it and removes her address book

Howard (*flicking through the pages*) Prescott ... Lawrence Prescott. (*He picks up the phone — but hesitates*)

Colin enters laden with garden tools: rake, spade, hoe, fork, etc.

Colin Knock, knock! Oh. Where is everyone?
Howard Upstairs showing him round.
Colin Ha! Going to buy it, is he?

Howard Hardly. It's half his, already.

Colin Is it? Yes, I suppose it is. Never thought of that. Quite right, of course.

Howard Did you want something, Colin?

Colin Um ... yes. An assortment of things here and I wondered ...

Howard Please, just take them.

Colin Good. Because, there's a bunch of disabled kids — just been given an allotment near us ...

Howard Colin, just have them. I'm sure Mother would be only too pleased.

Colin Right. Sorry. You're on the phone. (*Trying to be quiet, Colin blunders noisily into the hall*)

Howard considers the phone again but ...

(*Entering the living-room*) Howard?

Howard Yes, Colin.

Colin Sorry. As a matter of interest, what d'you think it's worth, this place?

Howard No idea. One-eighty, something like that.

Colin One hundred and eighty. My word. That's a hell of a camper.

Rachel comes down the stairs

Rachel Howard? Colin, what are you doing with those?

Colin (*meeting Rachel in the hall*) Putting them in the car.

Rachel We don't want all those; you've got a shedful at home.

Colin I know, but I was just explaining to Howard ——

Rachel (*taking the tools from Colin*) Come on, we've more important things to do than collect tools. (*She escorts Colin towards the front door*) Now listen. I want you to go into the estate agents up the road and check the house prices in ...

Rachel and Colin exit, Rachel's voice trailing off

Howard considers his phone call again and resolves to give it another try

Rachel returns through the front door, listens for voices upstairs and furtively makes for the living-room

Rachel Howard ...?

Howard clicks the phone off

Howard, before they come down — about the house. I think we ought to get it cleared up, don't you?

Howard Colin seems to be doing a good job.

Rachel I didn't mean that. I meant — you know — where he fits in.

Howard Who? ... Oh, how sweet. Can't quite bring yourself to say it, can you? You mean our father.

Rachel We can't afford to be sentimental about it. No need for a scene or anything.

Howard Sentimental about what?

Rachel Him — walking in here and claiming what's his. He can't — not after forty years.

Howard I think you'll find he can.

Rachel Well, we must get it cleared up. I'm sure he'll be the first to agree.

Howard Do you? I wish you luck.

Rachel All you have to do is broach it with him.

Howard I beg your pardon?

Rachel But, be nice about it, Howard. It's no use getting all ——

Howard You want me to tell this man he's out by about a hundred grand?

Rachel He'll be most understanding, I'm sure.

Howard Oh, fine ... (*He calls*) David!

Rachel Not like that! Don't be so stupid, Howard! Not just like that. Do it gently.

Howard Why me, as a matter of interest?

Rachel Because you're the eldest and his son and it's man's work. Now, come along and do your stuff. Quick, they're coming.

Frances and David appear on the stairs

Now, remember — be nice.

Frances leads David into the living-room. She pulls a face at the other two; clearly David has been a little overcome

Frances Here we are.

Rachel That's it. All the memories flooding back, I expect.

David Yes ... it's been a long time.

Frances Did you want to see the garden, or —— ?

Rachel Well, before you do that, before you do, Howard and I were just talking, weren't we, Howard? Well, we were and we were just discussing ... Well, you say, Howard, go on ... you say ... Howard.

Howard Rachel feels ——

Rachel The point is, David, it has been a long time, hasn't it?

David Very.

Rachel Quite. And ... after such a very long time, there's a lot to get used to, isn't there?

David Yes.

Rachel I knew you'd understand. You see, Howard? I said he'd understand.

David What are you trying to say, Rachel?

Rachel Sharing. I'm talking about sharing because ... there's lots of things we'd like to share with you, our children and so on. But some things ... it's going to be quite difficult to share, I think, don't you?

David Such as?

Howard The house. She's worried about the house.

David Whose house?

Howard This house. Or the money it fetches, anyway.

Rachel Not just me, we all are, Howard.

Howard Frankly, I couldn't give a ——

Rachel Oh, come on! You always did this — they always did this. "Come on, Rachel, let's go carol singing. That's it, ring the bell" — and flaming legged it. All five verses of "Come All Ye Faithful", all on my blooming tod!

David Look, perhaps I can help. We've reached this point sooner than I'd anticipated but ... no matter. Now, as far as the law's concerned, the issue's quite simple. You know the position, presumably.

Rachel Sort of. Howard does, or says he does, don't you, Howard?

Howard It's half his. I've told you: the house is in their joint names so one half of it's his. The other half comes to us as part of her estate. Yes?

David Er ... no. Not really.

Rachel The letter of the law Howard's talking about, aren't you Howard?

David Yes, I know. And the letter of the law is perfectly clear. If the deeds are in joint names, then when one partner dies the other gains sole ownership ... Did you not know that?

Rachel looks at Howard

Howard (*shaking his head knowingly*) Of course. Stupid of me.

David I'm sorry. I just assumed, as you'd brought the subject up, that you'd taken that on board.

Rachel Well, we hadn't.

David No. Dear me.

There is an awkward pause

Well, not to worry. Let's not allow it to get in the way of things.

Rachel Get in the ... ? It's been forty years!

Frances Rachel.

David I know it has, my dear.

Rachel Well, that's rather a long time, wouldn't you say?

David Yes, I would. Which is why, if you'll allow me ——

Frances Time! Grief! He'll be here any minute. (*She grabs a packet of labels from her bag*) Look, I'm through upstairs so I'll just quickly scoot round down here and label what I find.

Frances exits into the front room

Rachel So, that's it then, Howard; not even half.

Howard He's quite within his rights.

Rachel Is he. And the contents as well, I suppose?

Howard No, they're mostly Mother's so I imagine ...

Rachel The desk isn't. It was a gift from his aunt. So what do we do — go through item by item?

David Rachel, we've been discussing the law here.

Rachel I know we have! I know we're discussing the flaming law!

David As far as I'm concerned, everything belongs to you.

Rachel Oh, wonderful. You hear that, Howard? We can all retire now on Aunty Mildred's bloody desk!

Howard Rachel, shut up.

Rachel Well, I don't know about anyone else but I came here with a job to do and after that I've my children's tea to get. They have this strange disease, you know: twice a day their bellies contract, their mouths open and you have to shovel food down it. Apparently it's incurable.

David Rachel, could I just ...?

Rachel No, honestly. I'd love to chat but you know how it is with kids ... or perhaps you don't.

Frances enters from the front room

Rachel goes into the hall and collides with Frances

Frances Whoops! Where are you going in such a hurry?

Rachel Not Paris, that's for sure ... (*She heads up the stairs*) I'm going to grab what I can before any other dead relatives appear and start stripping the place of light fittings!

Rachel vanishes into an upstairs room and slams the door

There is a brief pause

Frances goes into the living-room

David Dear me. Not going too well this, is it?

Howard Not swimmingly, no.

Howard and Frances exchange a look. David appears awkward and embarrassed

David Perhaps if I take that stroll round the garden, when I come back we could start again. Yes, I think I'll do that.
Frances It's through ——
David I know the way; thank you.

David exits into the kitchen, heading for the garden

Frances Is there nothing we can do?
Howard Wouldn't have thought so; he's rock solid. Anyway, it's degrading.
Frances You can't blame him, either; it's a lot of money.

Colin enters through the front door leafing through sheets of estate agents' material

Colin I've got some, Rache! (*He enters the living-room*) Look at these — One ninety, two hundred ... (*He sees Howard and Frances but no Rachel*) Sorry. Rachel?
Frances Upstairs.
Colin Right. (*He bounds upstairs*) Rachel? Rachel!

Colin vanishes into the upstairs room

Frances Right. I think that's about it. Now, if I've labelled anything you want ...
Howard I'm really not bothered, Frances.
Frances No. Howard, before I disappear: this business with Rosemary.
Howard I'd rather not talk about it.
Frances You must have known, surely.
Howard There's knowing and knowing, isn't there?
Frances You people, you make all these damn promises to each other and ... well, thank God I never did it. Give me a dependable lover any day.

Rachel appears at the top of the stairs clutching the sheets of estate agents' material. Colin follows her on. Rachel rips the papers into small pieces. Colin watches, confused

Rachel Bless our home and those within it, watch over us, we pray! Keep our hearts and minds at peace — and chuck it down the drain! (*She lets the pieces flutter down into the hall*)

Rachel exits into the bedroom

Colin moves to follow but the door is slammed in his face. He hurries back downstairs

Colin What's going on?
Frances She's upset about the house. Apparently we don't even own it.
Colin Don't we? Who does, then?
Frances David.
Colin Who's ... ? Oh! Is that his name? Well, well. I never knew that. Mmmh. Bit of a blow that. Still, it's what I always say: you've no sooner got it than it's gone.

Rachel appears upstairs and throws a full bin-liner over the banisters

(*Calling up to Rachel*) Never mind eh, Rache! Still got the camper, haven't we?
Rachel Oh yes! With that and Aunty Mildred's desk we can set up in antiques!

Rachel vanishes, slamming the door again

Colin I'll go and talk to her. (*He bounds back upstairs*) Come on, Treasure — it's not the end of the world, is it?

Colin exits. Howard and Frances are alone again

Frances You'll at least ring her, won't you?
Howard Sorry?
Frances Rosemary.
Howard Oh. Maybe.
Frances Howard, you must.
Howard I'm no good at this sort of thing, Fran, I'm no good at it!
Frances You'd be no good on your own either. You'll end up in a singles bar and start wearing jeans or something. Please, Howard, it'll be awful. We'll find you wandering round Marks and Spencer's food department looking pathetic. Don't put us through all that.
Howard Just drop it, will you?
Frances (*looking in her bag*) Here ... you'll need the number. You can't ring her with ——
Howard Frances, I said drop it!

Rachel appears at the top of the stairs and throws two full bin-liners over the banisters to join the accumulating clutter in the hall. Rachel comes downstairs

Colin enters at the top of the stairs and follows Rachel down

Rachel Colin, you're a wonderful husband. You've always said we'll manage and we always have.
Colin There we are, then.
Rachel I don't want to manage! I'm sick of managing! (*She enters the living-room*) I want to be rich like these two. Look at her (*Frances*) — you could buy a new camper with what she's standing up in!

She exits to the kitchen

Colin Oh, don't be ... (*He takes a second look at Frances*) Mind you, I don't know — an ex-demonstration model, perhaps. Rachel?

Colin follows Rachel into the kitchen

Howard returns the phone to his briefcase and shuts it

Frances (*rummaging in her bag*) Funny ... Have you seen my address book? You gave it back to me earlier.

Howard pulls the small black book from his pocket and tosses it to her. He makes for the door with his briefcase

   Where are you going?
Howard To put this in the car.
Frances (*holding out the address book*) You still need the number.
Howard (*pointing to his brain*) I've got it. Don't worry.
Frances Howard?
Howard What?
Frances Just tell her you need her. We don't ask much — we're the fairer sex, remember?
Howard Fairer? The Marquess of Queensberry would turn in his grave.

Howard goes into the hall and exits through the front door

Colin and Rachel enter from the kitchen and move into the hall

Colin Now, that's not fair, Rachel — you've never wanted for anything.
Rachel Ha! (*She stumbles on the clutter in the hall*) Get this lot loaded, Colin, and then start on the door-knobs, finger-plates, the lot — I want nothing left.
Colin Come on, Rachel, you're just being silly.

Rachel (*going upstairs*) There's a mirror in the bathroom, too, and a toothbrush-holder — I want them all off!
Colin (*following Rachel*) Now look, Rachel —— !
Rachel Colin! Mandy'll be home in an hour — we haven't much time!

They vanish up the stairs

Frances begins making up her face in the mirror

David enters from the kitchen

David Stood the test of time pretty well. I should have thought two hundred was about right.
Frances Oh, what? Worth every penny.
David Now, then. Where is everyone?
Frances Howard's in the car and Rachel's upstairs. They'll be back in a minute.
David Fine. Not in your way, am I, if I hang on here?
Frances Not at all. If you don't mind watching a woman paint.
David It's a long time since I've had the privilege.

David studies Frances as she does her face with lipstick and mascara

David You never married, did you, Frances?
Frances Me? No. I've a weak stomach.
David Not much fun, is it — being on your own?
Frances Oh, I don't know. I have friends. Do you have friends, David?
David Yes.
Frances Nice, aren't they? You get to choose friends.
David You don't regret it, then?
Frances What?
David Never having found someone.
Frances Someone who what?
David Asked you to marry him.
Frances I did. He was kind and gentle and, oh, gorgeous! So attractive!
David What happened?
Frances He blew it.
David How?
Frances Silly idiot asked me to marry him.
David But, why didn't you say "yes"?
Frances Because I liked him.
David Is there nothing about marriage that appeals to you, nothing you miss?

Frances A good row, perhaps. I miss a husband for that. But I've an excellent solution. You know how some people sing to their house-plants? Well, I scream abuse at mine. And they're marvellous: they never slam doors and you don't have to apologize later.

Rachel appears at the top of the stairs, man-handling one end of a wardrobe. Colin is just visible at the other end. There is a frightful clattering noise as they head down the stairs

Colin Rachel, if you need a wardrobe, I'll buy you a wardrobe!
Rachel It's Mother's. It'll go on the roof-rack with the bags inside. Push, Colin!
Colin I am pushing!
David (*to Frances*) What on earth's going on?
Frances God knows. (*She goes into the hall*) Rachel, what *are* you doing?
Rachel Dancing — what does it look like? (*She squeezes past the wardrobe*) Damn it, I can't get back now. (*She climbs over the side of it*) Give me your hand, Colin.
Colin What?
Rachel Your hand! Pull, man ...

Colin pulls Rachel by the hand over the wardrobe

Ow!

Rachel vanishes upstairs

Frances (*returning to David*) Priceless, those two; someone should sell tickets.
David Will Howard be long, d'you think? I'd quite like to sort this out.
Frances Any second, I imagine.

Frances continues to make up. David observes her again

David Psychologists would say it was all my fault, of course.
Frances Nonsense. Rachel's a "coper" — she's not happy unless she's coping with something.
David I meant, you not getting married.
Frances Oh, that. Yes. Still ... (*She turns from the mirror*) ... too late now; well past my sell-by date. D'you think this blouse is a bit young for me?
David Children need a mother and a father.
Frances Well, this is true. No, I think I can get away with it — just.

David What I meant was — if I'd been around ——

Frances We'd have been all right. Instead of which there are three grotesque mutants running wild on the streets: a manic depressive son, the twisted remains of an unmarried hag ——

Rachel enters and tips a box of items noisily into the wardrobe on the stairs. She slams the wardrobe door and vanishes

— and a psychotic hen vandalizing your house upstairs.

David moves to call up to Rachel but is interrupted by Frances

We didn't need you, David.

David I wasn't there when it mattered, Frances.

Frances We're OK.

David That's not the point.

Frances Fine. We needed you desperately. (*She returns to the mirror to complete her make-up*)

There is a brief pause

Tell me something. Did you lie to my mother when you started seeing this other woman?

David Yes.

Frances What for?

David What for? To keep her from being hurt, I suppose.

Frances Ha! Brilliant. The wonders of masculine logic. And how did you fare on that score: quite good at them, were you? The porky-pies?

David She believed me.

Frances Really. I heard a terrific one the other day. What was it, now? Oh yes: "Sorry, darling. You know how it is — stuck in a pub with a few of the chaps." Out of nowhere. Inspired, I thought, and so original.

David I didn't enjoy lying to your mother.

Frances So, why didn't you tell her the truth?

David It would have utterly destroyed her.

Frances I see. So, to protect her and generally lift her spirits, you said you'd rather be trapped in a smoke-filled pub with some boring old farts from the office than stuck at home with her.

David To have told the truth would have helped matters, would it?

Frances Helped? She didn't want your help, you silly man. No-one wants to be helped.

David What, then?

Frances She wanted to win you back! And, if you'd come clean and let her, you wouldn't be in this mess to begin with.

David Really.

Frances No, stupid, because when you came back, she'd have done it. You'd have chosen her ... against Miss England nineteen-fifty.

David That's perverse.

Frances So is two-timing your wife and kids.

David All I wanted was to come home!

Frances Then why in God's name didn't you say so?

David I did!

Frances You didn't! You said "Hallo darling. I've come back to save you all from a terrible life without me"! It's a bloody insult. No woman should stand for that — and she didn't. Good for her.

David How dare you, Frances! You weren't there; I never said any such thing.

Frances No. And I'll bet you never told her you loved her, that you were wrong, that you liked being with her more, either. The choice, David; that's all she wanted to hear.

There is a pause

David Quite the little expert, aren't we?

Frances I've seen it all a hundred times.

David You know nothing. Nothing of marriage and nothing, I suspect, of love. A game, that's all it is to you.

Frances I've never spent time with a man who hadn't chosen to be there.

David Being there is easy, Frances. It's the staying that counts. And none of them do, do they, these men of yours? Not with you, at any rate.

There is a pause

Frances (*looking at David*) At least I'm not the one they lie to.

Rachel appears on the stairs

Rachel Frances!

Frances (*going into the hall*) Yes, Rachel. What is it?

Rachel Where's Howard?

Frances I don't know.

Rachel Well, find him.

Frances You find him.

Rachel I can't find him — I'm stuck up here!

Frances God ... (*She opens the front door*) Howard? (*She slams the front door*) It's all right, I've found him.

Rachel Where?

Frances Still in the car.

Rachel Then go and get him.

Frances He's busy, Rachel. He's talking to Rosemary.

Rachel What, in the car?

Frances On the phone in the car, yes.

Rachel Oh, typical! Typical Howard — he'd rather be reconciled with his wife than help!

The end of a curtain rail appears through a bedroom door

Keep that, Colin! I want those, and the hooks, and the curtain rail!

Rachel disappears upstairs

Frances returns to David

David I loved your mother.

Frances But you also had to be needed, didn't you?

David You seriously think if I'd phrased it differently none of this would have happened?

Frances Who knows? You're all the same, you marrieds. It's not what you do and say that causes the pain, it's what you don't do and don't say. Too many games. So much dishonesty ... (*She looks at her watch*) Grief, I've heard of cutting it fine but this is ridiculous. (*She packs her make-up away and zips up her bags*) I've seen those married men legging it to the station at six in the morning. The truth is, if they could catch an earlier train, they would. And the wives are no better: "Oh, my poor dear husband. The hours he works, we never seem to see each other." Give 'em half a chance they'd buy the network and run 'em all night.

Howard comes through the front door and stumbles into the mounting clutter in the hall

Howard, splendid; what news from the front?

Howard What? Oh, I told her quite plainly: I was prepared to have her back, to forget what's happened and carry on.

Frances Carry on?

Howard Where we left off.

Frances God, how depressing. I should think she jumped at that.

Howard She hung up.

Frances No! Really? You didn't, by any chance, tell her you needed her, did you?

Howard Of course I did. "You're far too old to be doing this, Rosemary," I said, "You need a home and you need me."

Rachel appears at the top of the stairs

Rachel Howard?
Howard What?
Frances I thought you said you needed her.
Howard I did.
Frances You didn't. You said ——
Howard I know what I said, Frances — don't split hairs with me. (*He enters the living-room*) So, that's it; nothing more I can do. If she wants to walk out on me, that's up to her. Her choice, her bed — she can damn well lie in it. I need a drink.
Frances (*following Howard*) You didn't speak to her at all, did you?
Howard No.
Frances You are a complete and utter arsehole, Howard.
Howard I'm no good at this, Frances, I've told you.
Frances Well, I give up. (*To David*) He's your son, you try. Now's your chance for some fatherly ... No, don't, actually. It takes practice.
Rachel Howard?
Frances Go and help her; she's been screaming for hours.
Howard What's she doing?
Frances I don't know ... (*She looks at her watch again*) This is insane! We're never going to make it!

Howard goes into the hall

(*Gathering her bags: to David*) Look, we'll keep in touch or something, yes?
David Please, Frances, before you rush off ——
Frances I can't. He's probably sitting outside in the car. (*She blows him a kiss*) Call me. And I'm sorry if I was a bit ... you know.
Howard (*calling up the stairs*) What the hell are you doing, Rachel?
Frances (*squeezing past Howard in the hall*) Sorry to dash, you lot.
Rachel Oh, not at all. You'll send us a postcard, won't you, to add to the collection?

Colin appears at the top of the stairs with a shower fitting in his hand

Colin This is stupid. What do we want a shower fitting for?
Rachel (*grabbing the fitting and stuffing it in the wardrobe*) Lift, Colin. Ready, Howard?
Frances Howard — speak to your wife.

Frances exits

Rachel Howard?

Howard Look, what are we doing, exactly?
Rachel Moving it down — come on.

Colin and Howard struggle with the wardrobe

Colin To you, Howard, and down a bit ... Bath plugs, curtain rails: anyone
would think we were gypsies.
Rachel Gypsies are rich; their campers are waterproof.
Colin There's food on the table and shoes on our children's feet!
Rachel Oh, shut up and push, Colin.

David wanders into the hall

David Good heavens — that old thing. Used to belong to my father.
Rachel I beg your pardon? (*To Colin*) Just a minute, Colin. (*To David*) Sorry.
What was that?
David Had it in his dressing-room.
Rachel This?
David Yes.
Rachel This wardrobe?
David Yes.
Rachel Belongs to you?
David Yes. Forgotten all about it.
Rachel Right. Back upstairs with it, Colin — and you, Howard. Quickly ...

Frances enters through the front door

Frances Howard, can I use your phone?
David Ah, good. Now, you're all together again I'd like, if I may, to have
a word.
Frances Howard?
Howard Yes, all right but you'll need the car keys.
Rachel Lift, Howard!
Howard (*to Frances*) Just let me do this.
David It's about the house. Can I just say that I think we got our wires a bit
crossed earlier.
Rachel And can I just say: isn't it time you were off? Being daylight, you
shouldn't be floating about at all.
David Look, what I would like is for you three to have it.

There is a pause. Colin, Howard and Rachel stare over the banisters at him

So if you could leave that for a moment and come downstairs? (*He leaves
the others and returns to the living-room*)

Rachel What did he just say? (*She pushes past Frances and goes down the stairs into the living room*)

Howard, Frances and Colin follow Rachel into the living-room, Colin bringing up the rear

Frances I don't know, something about the house. Keys, Howard: quickly. I need to ring my answer-machine ... God.

Howard (*to David*) It's a major asset — you can't afford to throw it away.

David I can't afford not to, and I'm not "throwing away" what I never planned to keep. I'm sorry if I misled you earlier but until you understood it was mine by right I had nothing to give you. I've waited a long time to do this.

Howard Do what — repay us?

David No. Just give you something. That's all.

Rachel I honestly don't know what to say — do you, Howard?

Howard No.

Frances It's very generous and I don't want to appear churlish but my weekend's about to disintegrate ... Howard?

Howard Mmmh?

Frances Keys!

Howard throws his car keys to Frances

Frances exits speedily through the front door

Excuse me. Sorry.

Rachel I feel awful now; all that carry-on earlier. I really ... quick, Colin, you're good on the one-liners.

Colin You could try "thank you".

Rachel Yes. Thank you ... Oh! I don't know whether to laugh or cry; I think I'll have a drink instead. Come on, let's all have a drink.

Howard So ... Just like that, eh? A few quid, a stroke of the pen and we're all one big happy family again.

Rachel (*pouring herself a drink*) I can't wait for you to meet the children. The look on their faces, Colin; can you imagine?

David It was something she never allowed me to do; not a card on your birthdays, a book token at Christmas — nothing.

Howard But now you can.

David Yes.

Howard Because she's not around to stop you.

Rachel Howard? What are you saying?

Howard What we should all say, Rachel: "Thank you but no thank you".

Rachel What? Oh, don't be so stupid. (*To David*) He's joking, take no notice.

Howard Forty years she spent keeping this man out, and in half an hour we let him in again? No way. Sorry, old man, nothing doing.

Rachel It's two hundred thousand pounds, Howard!

Howard Exactly: we don't come that cheap.

Rachel Oh for ...! Well, you speak for yourself, you can't speak for Fran and me.

David It's a gift from me to the three of you.

Rachel What, all three or none at all?

Howard Ha! He's greedy as well. He wants his full quota of Brownie points. Sorry Father, the confessional's closed — no more absolutions today.

Rachel Howard, you can't start ... God. Look Howard, listen to me a minute. I hate, I absolutely loathe, carpets. Your house may be full of them, high-class, all-wool, I'm sure it is, but they turn my stomach! And d'you know why? (*She reaches for Colin*) Because this fantastic little man, here ——

Colin Rachel.

Rachel Shut up, Colin. This bloody amazing creature has worked his backside off selling the damn things. We've had a sitting-room piled high and a toilet full of underlay. New carpets stink, Howard. We ate meals, went to bed, our children even went to school, smelling of damn carpets! They were a joke in the classroom: "Here come the thick-pile kids." Now, you may be rich enough to play around with money, you may have the cash to drag up the past and run a crusade, but we don't!

Howard It isn't right, Rachel.

Rachel Says who? They're your principles — you foot the bill.

Howard How? What d'you mean?

Rachel We'll come to an arrangement: he gives it to all three of us but Fran and I split it.

Howard (*to Colin*) Ha! She's sharp, your wife.

Rachel Help me Colin — I'm going to hit him in a minute.

Howard Who gave you away, Rachel, to Colin, in church?

Rachel He wasn't there! It wasn't his fault!

Howard Wasn't his fault ... Where's he been, this man? When the chain came off my bike, when you were captain of the netball team and Fran was caught smoking in the school lavatories: where the hell was he?

Rachel She shut him out!

Howard And you believe that, do you? Yes, of course you do: for that sort of money, you'll believe anything.

Rachel makes a grab at Howard but Colin restrains her

Colin Rachel! All right, that's enough. I know I'm just an appendage here but, in my view, none of this is worth it.

Rachel Shut up. Don't you start.

Colin Well, look at the state of you; no one's died, have they? Well, they have, I know, but ... what I mean is, now she's gone, it's only a house, isn't it?

Rachel It's worth a lot of money, Colin!

Colin I know it's worth a lot of money but it's not as though we need it, is it?

Rachel Oh my God.

Colin Pack it in. We won't starve. And, if Howard thinks for the old girl's sake it would be wrong to take it then, I have to say, I agree ... *(To David)* Sorry — no offence.

There is a pause

Rachel I'm going mad. I swear it's like finding yourself on another planet. We've got children, Colin — couldn't they use a leg up? Tricia's got a Neanderthal thug climbing down her blouse; she'll be married in a minute, God help her — if they don't eat each other first.

Colin I provide and we do all right.

Rachel I don't call going on holiday in a leaky camper "all right"! Or covering the damp patch in Jamie's bedroom with a Kylie Minogue poster "all right", either!

Colin Don't you!

Rachel No!

Colin Fine! Terrific! Glad that's out in the open, anyway.

Frances enters through the front door, slamming the door behind her. She kicks her bags in the hall and goes into the living-room

Frances Don't ask.

Rachel Something came up, did it?

Frances A message on my machine: "Sorry darling, you know how it is: stuck at home with the wife and family ... blah-blah-blah." What wife? What family? What is it with you lot; why don't you tell the bloody truth?

Colin Come on, Rachel, it's time we got back for Jamie and Mandy.

Rachel Not until this is sorted out. Howard's gone all high-minded about the house, Fran. Howard thinks we shouldn't accept it.

Frances Oh? Why's that?

Rachel Because Howard thinks it's wrong.

Frances For who?

Rachel For us, for him, I don't know. He's ceased talking sense to me.

Howard *(referring to David)* He's after a trade: this house for an absolution.

David That really isn't true, you know.

Colin Rachel. We're late, it's raining, the kids'll be on the doorstep.
Rachel Then let them!
Colin (*ripping off his boiler suit*) Oh, fine. Suit yourself.
David Look. I came here today expecting nothing. The house was a matter
   of urgency because if the law runs its course you'll end up with nothing.
   To prevent that I had to present myself. This I have done. All I ask is now
   that you receive it. I can't give it to you if you won't take it! Please?

*There is a pause. Rachel looks from Howard to David and then from Frances
to David. There is no response*

Colin (*stuffing his boiler suit into a carrier bag*) Right then. (*He offers his
   hand to David*) Nice meeting you. Hopefully we'll see you again.
Rachel Colin, this won't take a minute!
Colin We don't have a minute, Rachel — our children are standing out in
   the rain!
Rachel They won't rust, will they?
Colin (*heading for the front door*) No, they won't rust ... By the way, if
   there's no-one in when you get home, don't panic: I'll be doing a stint on
   the petrol pumps, Tricia'll be on the streets and Jamie and Mandy'll be
   flogging glue — ten p a sniff in the back alley ... Every little bit helps!

Colin exits, slamming the front door behind him

*There is a pause. Howard, Rachel and Frances sit silently brooding. David
observes them*

Frances (*moving to look out of the window*) Well we must do this more often
   — try and make it a regular thing.
David Funny ... you spend years picturing a certain moment, imagining how
   it will be.
Howard The fatted calf being killed for the prodigal father, mmmh?
Rachel You're making this very difficult, Howard. He wants to give us
   something; let him, for God's sake!
Frances Our mother's integrity — is that what you're saying? What stands
   between us and his gift is her pride and impunity.
Howard She was a woman of principle, she never allowed him ——
Frances Yes, yes — but if it weren't for that, you'd gladly accept?
Howard Of course I would but it's hypothetical.
Frances Not really.

There is a pause

Rachel Fran? Oh God, she's at it again, Howard — she knows something. Well, come on "deep throat": what is it this time?

Frances It's important to you, David, isn't it, that we allow you to give us this house?

David It would mean a great deal to me.

Frances An expensive gift.

David I'm aware of the cost.

Frances I'm not talking about money. You know what I'm talking about, don't you?

Rachel Come on, Fran, spit it out. Where's her handbag? Pass it, Howard, I'm sure she's going to need it.

Frances I'm not his daughter.

There is a pause

Howard (*bursting into laughter*) Oh, don't be ridiculous, Frances. She was pregnant with you before he left.

Frances Precisely. She wasn't the paragon of virtue you imagine.

Rachel Hold on — this is another Plymouth. If she was pregnant but he hadn't yet left, how could anyone else be the ...? Unless ... God, whose was it, then?

Frances Not "it", Rachel: it's me we're talking about. While he was supposedly "working late", she was on the "early shift" being consoled by Uncle Nev.

Rachel Uncle Nev? But he played cricket! He had a car with smelly seats! He played cricket with Howard out there on the grass!

Frances I'm sorry, David. Did you really not know?

There is a pause

Howard Well, come on, did you or didn't you?

David Not about Frances. I'd always assumed she was mine ... Well, it was possible — let's put it that way. But I knew what your mother was up to — of course I knew.

Howard You actually knew?

David You can't keep a thing like that from your husband, Howard.

Howard Then, why the hell didn't you do something?

David Like what? What could I possibly do?

Howard Confront her, speak to the woman!

Frances They were man and wife, Howard, living together under the same roof. And up to their eyes in silence.

Rachel When did you discover all this, Frances?

Frances After Neville died. She had to tell me because he'd left me some money. That's how I got my business going. Anyway, there it is, Howard; you can lay down your torch now. You can't champion her innocence anymore.

Howard It's obvious why, of course.

Frances I beg your pardon?

Howard Why she did it. You could hardly blame her.

Frances Oh God! Just leave it now!

Howard Poor woman. Driven to it, I expect.

Frances What, forced you mean? No alternative? Strapped herself down and yelled "Take me, Nev — it's the only way to get him back!" from the upstairs bedroom?

Howard Don't be disgusting, Frances; you know perfectly well what I'm talking about.

Frances I don't, actually, and neither do you. Who lied to who, first? Did she jump or was she pushed? I don't know, you don't know. The point is: she did it ... and so did he. They lied to themselves and they lied to each other — and they've kept their mouths shut ever since.

Howard Nevertheless ...

Frances Nevertheless, they spent forty years not talking about it, Howard — forty years! I wouldn't wish that on anyone. Would you? Let him give you his precious house — and let's leave him in peace. And let's all of us mind our own business.

Howard gets up and moves towards the hall

Rachel Where are you going?

Howard It's stifling in here — I need some air.

Howard opens the front door

Colin is on the doorstep with Howard's mobile phone

Colin Ah, Howard ...

Howard Excuse me.

Howard exits

Colin enters the hall sheepishly

Rachel Colin — is that you? ...What are you doing?

Colin (*entering the living-room*) I phoned Mrs Bundock; she's got a key so I asked her to let Mandy in and keep an eye until Tricia gets back. Rachel ——

Rachel It's all right. It's all sorted out now. At least, I think it is.
Frances I would think so.
Rachel (*kissing David*) Thank you. I'm sorry. And I'm sorry we ... Colin, what are you doing with Howard's phone?
Colin Mmmh? Oh, blimey, I almost forgot ...

Howard storms in through the front door

Howard Would you believe it? My car's been broken into! (*To Colin, referring to the phone*) What are you doing with that?
Colin Sorry. It was flashing and ringing and the door was open.

Howard snatches the phone back

Sorry.

Howard turns to go

It's Rosemary, by the way.
Howard I beg your pardon?
Colin Rosemary.
Howard Where?
Colin There ... (*He takes the phone back*) He's here now, Rosemary — I've found him for you. (*He thrusts the phone back at Howard*)

Howard looks at the phone, takes it uncertainly and then exits through the front door

Frances Now, let's hope he's got the sense to go and fetch her.
Colin Well, he hasn't got far to go — she's only in a call-box up the road.
Frances What?
Colin She was queueing while I was on to Mrs Bundock and when I got to his car, there she was again on the end of his phone. "We can't keep meeting like this, Rosemary," I said, "Howard might suspect." Ha! ... No, she didn't find it funny, either. Anyway, the kids are all right, Rachel, so why don't we all go out?
Frances I can't, I'm afraid, I'm having dinner with someone already. (*She looks in her bag*) But somewhere in here, I've got these plane tickets so why don't you two —
Colin Ha! No, that's sweet of you ...!
Rachel Oh, we couldn't, Fran — not just like that!
Frances (*producing two tickets*) Oh, don't be so wet. There's at least two more flights out of Heathrow tonight and if you smile sweetly at the check-in desk ... (*She holds the tickets over the bin*) Well, it's that or the bin; there's no refund.

Rachel (*after a deep breath*) Oh, come on, Colin: let's do it. (*She hugs Frances*) Thank you, you're a wonderful sister ... No, wait a minute, you're not, are you? Are you? Yes, you must be ... Heavens, I'm so confused.

Frances I'm still your sister, Rachel, but I'm only half the sister you thought I was.

Rachel Good. So, nothing's changed, then ... (*To David*) You will come and see us, won't you?

David Thank you. I'd like that.

Colin Rachel, I'm not at all sure about this.

Rachel Oh, shut up Colin and live a little.

Colin (*heading for the front door*) But we need passports — and what about the kids?

Rachel (*following Colin*) We'll get passports and Tricia'll cope. Now, come on.

Colin But why don't we do it properly? Why don't we take the camper?

They exit, slamming the front door behind them

Frances returns to the mirror. She touches up her face again with make-up and tissues. David picks up the newspaper, folds it and puts it in his pocket

Frances Oh, this wretched mascara — I've got lashes like a portcullis.

David He was a good man, your father, Frances.

Frances Was he?

David We used to sail a lot together.

Frances Old chums, eh? Hopped it pretty smartish after I was born, didn't he?

David Yes. Odd that. I knew he'd gone, of course, but, under the circumstances, most out of character. Always such an upright sort of fellow ...

Frances (*turning from the mirror*) David ... The penny still hasn't dropped, has it?

David What penny?

Frances Why my father left the country. She asked him to. She was waiting for you. She knew you'd know he'd finally gone so she sat there ... waiting.

David But she had an address. She could find me. I told her, if she ever needed me ...

Frances Needed you? She loved you, you silly man. So, she waited ... and she waited .... and she waited.

David sits in the wing chair, silently overcome. He fumbles in his pocket. Frances hands him a tissue

Brave faces have a lot to answer for, don't they?

David Thank you ... Stupid ... Forgive me.

Frances Got lipstick on you now. (*She wipes his face*) ... Why doesn't anyone tell the truth any more?
David God knows.
Frances You'd have thought it was simple, wouldn't you?
David Perhaps that's why it's so difficult.

Howard enters tentatively through the front door

Howard I left some clothes. I need to collect them.
Frances Fine.
Howard (*gathering up his suit on its hanger*) I also came to say goodbye — well, not "goodbye-goodbye", just goodbye ... you know.
David Goodbye, Howard.
Howard Been one of those days, hasn't it?
David Yes, it has rather. Could have been a lot more painful.
Howard Could it?
David Oh yes — strangers engaged in polite conversation.
Howard Well, I'll be off. Oh, one thing. (*He searches around*) That newspaper, her crossword, I'd like to ... Where is it? It was here earlier ...
David (*reaching into his pocket and pulling out the newspaper*) This one, you mean?
Howard Yes. Did you ...?
David Can I?
Howard Do. Please. Well, cheerio, then.
Frances Howard?
Howard Mmmh?
Frances Is Rosemary with you?
Howard Yes. She's fine. (*He starts to go and then returns*) Well, she isn't actually. I mean, she is but she's not feeling too hot. Sends her apologies.
Frances Oh dear. I'm sure it's nothing that a warm bath and early night won't cure.
Howard Quite. Back trouble or something. Cheery-bye, then.

Howard shuffles off

Frances shuts the window. David stands and takes in the room and the wing chair

David She's been a step ahead of us all day, you know.
Frances Yes. I think she probably has. Right. Will I do? It's as good as it gets, I'm afraid.
David Delightful. The image of your mother. What time are you meeting this man?
Frances How d'you know it's a man?

David A wild guess.

Frances I'm not the predator they make me out to be; they just like having someone to look up to. I'm spending the evening with an old friend. That's all.

David Old friends are the best kind.

Frances Quite. (*She closes the curtains*) And you get to choose friends, don't you? Shall we go?

David How d'you mean? Go where?

Frances Somewhere quiet we can drink to the past.

They exit, pulling the front door shut behind them

The Lights fade slowly, a single spot lingering for a moment on the empty wing chair as ——

—— *the* CURTAIN *falls*

FURNITURE AND PROPERTY LIST

ACT I

On stage: LIVING-ROOM
Wing chair. *On it*: newspaper, pen
Small table. *On it*: cup and saucer
Bureau desk. *On it*: papers, postcard
Sofa
Mirror
Photographs, books, family memorabilia

HALL
Telephone table. *On it*: telephone, notepad, directories
Various newspapers, circulars, assorted pieces of useless debris

Off stage: Small bag (**Howard**)
Overnight bag and handbag containing black address book,
make-up, labels, tissues (**Frances**)
Two carrier bags. *In one*: housecoat (**Rachel**)
Hanger for Howard's suit (**Howard**)
Tray of tea things (**Rachel**)
Apron (**Frances**)
Hoover and bag containing boiler suit (**Colin**)
Flymo hover mower (**Colin**)
Cardboard boxes (**Howard**)
Briefcase containing letter (**Howard**)
Portable phone (**Howard**)
Full bin liners (**Frances** and **Rachel**)
Seed boxes and pot plants (**Colin**)
Can of spray polish, duster (**Rachel**)
Bag containing brandy and sherry bottles and nibbles (**Colin**)

ACT II

Off stage: Tray. *On it:* five champagne glasses (**Colin**)
Rake, spade, hoe, fork and other garden tools (**Colin**)
Sheets of estate agents' material (**Colin**)
Two full bin liners (**Rachel**)
Wardrobe (**Rachel** and **Colin**)
Clothes rail (**Stage Management**)
Box full of bric-a-brac (**Rachel**)
Shower fitting (**Colin**)

LIGHTING PLOT

ACT I

To open: Dim interior light, bright exterior light shining through curtains

Cue 1   **Frances** draws the curtains open   (Page 2)
           Bring up interior lights

ACT II

To open: As end of ACT I; darkening during ACT II to denote rain beginning
    by page 60

Cue 2   **Frances** and **David** exit   (Page 66)
           Slow fade, spot lingering on wing chair

EFFECTS PLOT

ACT I

Cue 1   **Rachel** exits upstairs   (Page 23)
          Flymo starts up in garden

Cue 2   **Colin**: "Sorry! Sorry!"   (Page 23)
          Flymo sound dies away

Cue 3   **Howard**: "'... from the smoke', the postcard said." (Page 24)
          Mobile phone rings

Cue 4   **Frances**: "... obliged to do something, won't you?" (Page 27)
          Mobile phone rings

Cue 5   **Rachel** takes a swig from the brandy bottle   (Page 35)
          Doorbell rings

ACT II

No cues

MADE AND PRINTED IN GREAT BRITAIN BY
LATIMER TREND & COMPANY LTD PLYMOUTH
MADE IN ENGLAND